PARMA

Art, history and monuments

EDITION

officina grafica bolognese S.R.L.

info@ogbsrl.it

© **Copyright 2012 by OGB Officina Grafica Bolognese Srl**
Via Augusto Pollastri, 22 - 40138 Bologna - Italia Tel. +39 051 532 203 - Fax +39 051 532 188
e-mail: info@ogbsrl.it - www.ogbsrl.it

Text, layout and printed in UE by OGB Officina Grafica Bolognese Srl - Bologna - Italy

Photos by: Foto Amoretti, P. Candelari, Foto Furoncoli, Archivio OGB Officina Grafica Bolognese Srl

ISBN: 9788860780171

PARMA

Parma is located north of the Apennines and south of the Po River, right in between. It was founded by the Romans on 183 BC on a pre-existent Celtic settlement to complete the occupation and defence schedule of the Via Aemilia, which ran already from Piacenza to Rimini. Although destroyed during the war between the Roman Emperor Octavian Augustus and Anthony, Parma soon flourished again thanks to the fertility of the surrounding area and the strategic position it had in the existing road network of the times, completed by a bridge that Augustus built in the city. It thus became a flourishing commercial centre both for foodstuff and textures. After Augustus' death in 14 AD, a slow decadence began that led to the conquer of the city at first by the Huns in the 5th century and then by the Etruscans. In the first part of the 6th century, under Theodoric's rule and then under the Byzantine Empire, the city experienced a slight reprise that was interrupted in 570 by the invasion of the Lombards, who elected a Duke to rule it. This domination lasted for about two centuries, until Charlemagne proclaimed himself King of the Franks and the Lombards in 774 after having defeated King Desiderius in Pavia that same year. Under Frank rule Parma was elected as Capital of the countryside and was ruled by a Count. Between the 10th and 12th century the rule of the city passed to the Church. The Bishops that followed on to rule the city gave a strong impulse to public education founding the *Chapter of the Cathedral*, which became a strong cultural centre and certainly gave birth to the University of Parma, one of Italy's most ancient universities. The construction of the Bishop's Palace and of the Cathedral (1092), sided by the Presbytery, date back to this period. The latter faces the current *Piazza Duomo*, which was completed as city centre in 1196, when the construction of the Baptistery began in the South side. It was terminated only in 1270. These three buildings where built in Romanesque style, moving from the simple one of the Bishop's residence to the more refined one of the Baptistery, built almost two centuries later. The Church's temporal power was eventually broken by Frederick I, known as *Barbarossa*, who imposed his representative, called *Podestà,* as ruler of the city.

The various free cities of the Po Valley rebelled to the greedy imperial fiscal system and a coalition of their armies finally and definitely defeated the Imperial army in Legnano, in 1176. The municipal form of government established before the Church's temporal rule was somehow maintained by the Bishops and *Barbarossa*, but it reached its real independence only after the League of the Free Cities of the Po Valley beat the Emperor in Lugano. Frederick II Hoenstaufen, the nephew of *Barbarossa*, came to Italy in 1220 to reinstate Imperial power but was driven away after his defeat in Parma in 1248 by a league of free cities backed up by the Church. For a certain period the rule of the city changed from the form of Commune composed by several Consuls to that of Seigniory, held by a single person. In 1346 the Visconti conquered Parma and dominated it until 1447. After two years of independence, Parma passed under the rule of the Sforza, who maintained their power on the city until 1449. During the domination by these two families, Parma, located at the borders of the duchy, was fortified with the construction of castles on the two sides of the river splitting the city. Castles were built also outside the city. Having dwelling as well as defensive purposes, they were given elegant shapes, with furniture and frescoes worthy of the courts that dwelled in them. The Castles of S. Secondo, of Torrechiara and of Roccabianca date back to these years.

From the end of the 15th century until the mid-16th, when the Farnese conquered the city, Parma was the theatre of battles between the latter, who had taken the whole Duchy of Milan from the Sforza, and the Spaniards that were supporting the Papacy. During these years the Renaissance reached even Parma. *Correggio* and *Parmigianino* were among its major representatives for painting, while sculpture had virtually no followers. In 1545, Pope Paul III _ in the world Alessandro Farnese _ created the Duchy of Parma and Piacenza and gave its rule to his son Pier Luigi, in accordance with a previous agreement with Emperor Charles

V. This caused hostility by the Este and the Gonzaga, who ruled the nearby Ferrara and Mantova, as well as by the Emperor himself together with the aristocracy of Parma. The latter, tired with Pier Luigi's power, had him killed in 1547 in Piacenza to regain the rule of its land, which he had dismembered.

A new ruling class was created favouring the middle class and the common people. The Farnese's rule on the city lasted for 185 years, with 8 dukes reaching power one after the other.

Pier Luigi was followed by Ottavio (1547-1586), who in 1561 decided the construction of the *Palace of the Garden* located across the stream, probably on a design by *Vignola*. When he died he was followed by his son Alessandro who left the regency to his son Ranuccio I in 1592, because the Emperor Philip II had appointed him Governor of the

the immense complex of the *Pilotta* _ a symbol of his absolute power and obscure character _ on a previous building by the Sforza. He also ordered the construction of the Theatre and of powerful walls, to complete the *Cittadella*. A cultured man, he founded the *College of Nobles,* and entrusted it to the Jesuits. In 1612 he had the alleged conspirators _ a group of feudatories willing to rebel to his despotism _ ruthlessly killed. The small 10 year-old son Odoardo succeeded him under the regency of his Uncle Cardinal Odoardo and his mother Margherita Aldobrandini. In 1628 he married Margherita de' Medici. On the occasion he opened the Theatre, and had the Palace of the Commune *rebuilt.* The latter had been destroyed in 1606 by the collapse of the tower. He died young, in 1646, and was succeeded by the son *Ranuccio II* who reigned until 1694 and continued the wars that the father Odoardo had began against the Barberini, who thus re-conquered the Duchies of Castro and Ronciglione. In 1662, he founded the *Academy of the Chosen Ones.*

The son Francesco Maria succeeded him and reigned until 1727. Lacking sons, he was succeeded by the brother Antonio, who died only 4 years later in 1731. He was also without sons, thus the Farnese dynasty died out and the Duchy's rule passed on to Charles of Bourbon, the son of Elisabetta Farnese and Philip V, as agreed in 1720 with the treaty of the Hague. He took office in Parma in 1732 but left after two years for Naples, which he had conquered in the meantime, and took with him many of the furnishings and collections that had been stored in the various Ducal palaces _ among which the Farnese library stood out. In 1736, he gave up the Duchy to Austria, and such annexation was made official with the treaty of Vienna in 1738. In 1748, with the peace of Aachen the Duchy returned to the Bourbons enriched with the Duchy of Guastalla, in the person of Philip, the second-born brother of Charles.

Netherlands. During the few years of his reign Alessandro, a great general and an expert in fortifications, decided in 1591 the construction of the *Cittadella,* a powerful building with a pentagon base. One of the reasons for this decision was the need to create jobs for the people, who had been reduced to starvation by the succession of wars, famines and epidemics. The son Ranuccio, who reigned until 1622, decided to build

Aerial view.
In the foreground Garibaldi Palace; in the background the Baptistery and the Cathedral

The wife Louise Elisabeth, the daughter of Luis V of France, summoned artists and craftsmen from Paris to restore at least part of the patrimony Charles had taken with him when he moved to Naples.

In any case, the Duchy was in precarious conditions, and only the work of *William du Tillot,* appointed prime minister in 1759, managed to lift it both economically and culturally thanks to the privileged relationships he had with the powerful reign of France. He surrounded himself with intellectuals, even foreign ones, and founded the *Academy of Fine Arts, the Palatina Library,* the *Antiquity Museum* and the *Royal Printing Works*, taking advantage of the presence of *Bodoni* in Parma.

He fought against the privileges the Papacy had acquired during the centuries, he drove off the Jesuits that dominated education in the Duchy, and reformed the University.

Duke Philip died of smallpox in 1765, and the son Ferdinand, who succeeded him to the throne, dismissed Tillot. This caused the breaking up also of the group of intellectuals that had helped him in his enlightened reforming work.

Thanks to the works of the artists summoned to Court, the period of Bourbon domination left notable traces of French culture and taste in Parma, especially under the rule of Du Tillot. The contribution of the Architect *Alexandre Petitot* was notable. He gave impulse to urban renewing by restructuring the royal palaces of Parma and Colorno, the Ducal Palace and the Church of St. Peter, which was completely turned around by moving the facade on the square where the apse had been previously.

Moreover, he built the *Stradone*, at the end of which he built the *Casinò* as a resting and conversation place at the borders of the city.

In 1796, Napoleon took the Duchy, although he left Ferdinand to reign until his death in 1802.

Napoleon then entrusted the administration of the Duchy to *Moreau de Saint Mèry* who took the example of his predecessor and fellow-countryman Du Tillot and continued the secularization work by reforming the penal and civil codes and applying the new Napoleonic legislation.

In 1808 the Duchy was annexed to the French Empire as *Department of Taro*. In 1815 the Congress of Vienna sanctioned the assignation of the Duchy to *Marie Louise,* Napoleon's wife and Francis I of Austria's daughter, with the clause that once she died the Duchy would have been given back to the Bourbons of Parma, who in the meantime had obtained the Kingdom of Lucca.

In the first years Marie Louise reigned with the aid of the *Regent, Francesco Megalwi-Cerati*. The main purpose of her government was to help the population in recovering from the heavy economical crisis, while resuming relations with the religious organizations.

When Napoleon died, she remarried with *General Neipperg.* The Court of Vienna imposed the marriage to rule the Duchy according to its directives, while at the same time dismantling the Napoleonic code.

In 1847 the Duchess died and left an unfillable void in her subjects, who had appreci-

ated her human gifts and her ruling skills. In fact Marie Louise left her personal hallmark in Parma even in the architectural restoration of the urban texture, thanks to the precious co-operation of the architect *Nicola Bettoli*, one of the main representatives of the Neo-classic style.

They are responsible for the construction of the *Royal Theatre,* the *Beccherie* and the *Foro Boario* and for the reordering of the *Art Gallery,* of the *Palatina Library* and of many churches.

Once Marie Louise was dead, the Duchy returned to the Bourbons in the person of *Charles Ludovick*, who failed in giving a personal hallmark to his reign and abdicated after two years in favour of son *Charles III* who militarized the city and used various monasteries and part of the Pilotta as barracks. He was killed in 1854 just for the hatred he had arisen in all the social classes of the city with his politics aimed only at war. The son Robert I succeeded him, still a boy,

under the regency of mother *Louise Marie* of *Berry*. The latter distinguished herself for her enlightened politics aimed at getting people to forget that of her husband Charles.

She is responsible for the construction of the *Via della Salute*, across the stream, which was supposed to be the first core of a *district* created to give decent housing to the working class.

She was overwhelmed by the independence rising and abdicated in 1859 leaving Parma. Thanks to general elections, the following year the city was annexed to the Kingdom of Italy.

1: *Scenery with view of the Baptistery and the Bell Tower of the Cathedral.*
2: *Scenery with view of the Dome of the Church of the Steccata.*

1

2

A) PIAZZA GARIBALDI

It's the former *Piazza Grande*, and has always been the heart of the city. Many important buildings built from the 13th to the 16th century face it.

It underwent several changes, also following natural events such as the destruction of the old Palace of the Commune caused by the collapsing of a tower. The current look is the one given it by the architect *Petitot*.

B) PALACE OF THE GOVERNOR

The first foundation dates back to the last years of the 13th century, a fact stated also by two memorial slabs.

Two distinct bodies separated by Vicolo S. Marco originally composed it. The latter was changed into the current central vault in 1673, when the Communal Tower was built. It owes its current appearance to the architect Petitot who restored it in 1760, also creating the niche in the bell tower where the *Madonna with Child* by *Jean Baptiste Boudard* was placed.

The sun dials where executed in 1829 by *Lorenzo Ferrari*. The prototype of the *Parmesan* brick can be found on the corner with *Via Cavour*.

C) PALACE OF THE PODESTÀ

The first foundation dates back to the mid-13th century.

The palace consists of two bodies and features a wide vault and a series of elegant three-light windows, some of which ascending as they were following the steps of a large stairway that no longer exists.

D) PALACE OF THE COMMUNE

It was rebuilt in 1627, on the occasion of the wedding between *Odoardo Farnese* and *Margherita de' Medici,* on a project by *G. Battista Magnani* on the ruins of the *Palace of the Captain,* built in 1221 by *Torello di Strada.* The rectangular-planned building has a wide and high portico whose arches where opened in 1770, after it was decided to use the premises as barracks, salt customs

1: The Palazzo of the Governor
2: The Palaces of the Commune and of the Podestà

9

warehouse and mint. On the pillars it's possible to admire a bust of *Giuseppe Mazzini* and a bronze group by *T. A. Vanderstoch* depicting the *fight between Hercules and Antaeus* placed on a fountain designed by *Paolo Toschi*. The facade is covered with exposed fired-bricks.

A large stairway refurbished in 1887 leads to the *Council Hall,* preceded by an atrium where we can admire large paintings by *Ilario Spolverini* executed between 1715 and 1720, depicting the *Naumachia,* the large seats of the *Office of Elder*, a *Crucifixion attributed* to *Bernardino Gatti,* and the *Noli me tangere* attributed to *Annibale Carraci*.

The *Council Hall* bears frescoes of the 19th century executed by *Girolamo Magnani*. It also accommodates another two large paintings by Spolverini depicting: *The bridal procession of Elisabetta Farnese* and *The ceremony of her wedding in the Cathedral.*

E) FAINARDI PALACE

This building dates back to the 13th century as well, with later modifications. Only a few restored remains of the original building are left.

During the period of the Commune and of the Farnese the building was famous for its unhappy associations, because it was the seat of the Criminal Court, of the prison and of a room called *the Curlo* where death sentences were executed. For this reason it was known as the *Palace of Torment.*

During the 18th century the Court was transferred elsewhere, and the state sold the palace to private citizens who changed it internally and externally.

F) CHURCH OF ST. PETER

It was first built in the 9th century and a first reconstruction began in the first years of the 16th century. It terminated only two centuries later, reversing its orientation in order to have the facade facing the square, which used to be faced by the apse.

On the occasion the presbytery and the dome were risen and the chapels were widened, but the facade was left uncompleted. *Ottavio* and *Giovanni Bettoli* terminated the latter in Neo-classic style only in 1762, on a project by the architect *Petitot*, while restructuring the whole square.

The architect also designed the portal, made by the carver *Marc Vibert,* and the stucco decoration depicting the Pontifical coat of arms, made by *Benigno Bossi.*

The four Corinthian columns beside the portal are imposing, while a coffered dome surmounts the portal itself.

The church was painted yellow like the other palaces facing the square. Later on, yellow was adopted as colour of the Municipal Coat of Arms together with azure.

G) CHURCH OF ST. VITALIS

The first foundation is said to date back to the first years of the 10th century. In any case, the Church was completely rebuilt between 1651 and 1658 on a design by the architect *Cristoforo Rangoni,* known as *Ficarelli.*

The architect *Domenico Valmagini* rearranged the dome in 1676.

The facade is divided by a cornice and pilaster strips, between which the statues of four Saints are placed in niches underneath, and the statues of S. Vitalis and his wife S. Valerie above.

The inside has the shape of a single-nave Latin cross, with five chapels per side. On the central portal there is a large painting executed in 1832 by *Giovanni Tebaldi* depicting *St. Gregory praying for the souls of the Purgatory.* Two nice paintings surmount the lateral portals; the ten chapels display various paintings, stuccoes and decorations executed by local artists between the 16th and 19th centuries. Among these we would like to mention the large stucco decorating the fifth chapel on the left, placed in the transept dedicated to the *Madonna of Constantinople* that is depicted in a painting overlooking the altar.

Domenico and *Leonardo Reti* realized the stuccoes between 1666 and 1669, on commission by *Carlo Beccaria*, the treasurer of the Farnese.

The presbytery, the high altar and the large niche were designed and partly realized by *Pietro Righini. Giuseppe Peroni* frescoed the bowl-shaped vault and the vault in 1760 by depicting the *Passing away of S. Vitalis,* the *Triumph of Religion* and *biblical scenes.*

The prevailing style in the Church *is* Baroque.

H) CHURCH OF ST. MARY OF THE STECCATA

This elegant Renaissance Church owes its strange name to the fact that towards the end of the 19th century there was a house nearby bearing a painted image of *St. John*

the Baptist that was considered miraculous; a fence (*steccata*) was then raised to contain the crowd that used to gather in front of it. In 1392 an Oratory was erected in honour of St. John where a *Madonna feeding the Child* was painted. The people immediately called it *The Blessed Virgin of the Steccata.*

In 1521 the oratory was demolished and the construction of the new imposing building began to celebrate the victory on the French _ also thanks to the Commune's and the people's financial support. The first works up to the cornice where taken care of by *Bernardino Zaccagni* and the son *Gian Francesco.* They where dismissed in 1525 due to contrasts with the commissions controlling the works.

Construction was resumed under *Marcantonio Zucchi's* guidance and eventually finished in 1539 under *Gian Francesco D'Agrate*, who also realized the marble works.

1: *T. A. Vanderstoren: The fight between Hercules and Antaeus. The fountain is a work by Paolo Toschi*
2: *The Church of St. Peter*
3: *Church of the Steccata. The entrance with the Coat of Arms of the Order of St. Giusto*

3

The luminous dome was realized following the design of *Antonio da Sangallo il giovane,* a pupil of *Bramante*, summoned to Parma to give advice on the construction of this Church and some defensive works.

External finishing works were performed between 1695 and 1697 by *Mauro Oddi,* and thirty years later the architect *Adalberto della Nave* took care among other things of the construction of the new choir of the *Knights of St. George*, as the Church had become since 1725 the seat of their Order; the Order's coat of arms, supported by two angels, appears on the main portal.

The inside has the form of a Greek cross and displays four chapels obtained at the limits of the arms of the cross. It's enriched with countless painted decorations, among which the one on the large arch of the presbytery stands out. It is a real masterpiece realized by *Parmigianino* between 1530 and 1539.

In the bowl shaped vault on the entrance it's possible to admire the *Adoration of the Magi*, a fresco by *Michelangelo Anselmi* who started it in 1548 but couldn't finish it because of his death in 1555. *Bernardino Gatti* finished the edges of the work in 1559.

The two large paintings on the wall are a work of *Parmigianino;* their edges were also completed by another artist, *Gerolamo Mazzola Bedoli*, and eventually restored in 1580 by *John Sons.*The large arch was decorated by *Michelangelo Anselmi:* the right hand side depicts *Truth and Innocence*, while the left hand side shows *Justice* between Peace and a feminine figure.

The games of the putti decorating the two final friezes are a work by *Bernardino Gatti*. The marble sculptures on the right are the *Pietà*, realized in 1845 by *Tommaso Bandini* on order by *Marie Louise,* and *Our Lady of Sorrows*, a work by *Guastalla*. The funereal monument of Count *Adam Neipperg*, *Marie Louise's* husband, is a work of *Lorenzo Bartolini*.

The first chapel on the right has beautiful marble walls by *Gian Francesco D'Agrate* and

Church of St. Mary of the Steccata
1: The imposing mass
2: The Atrium and the inside: note the large arch by Parmigianino between the frescoed dome by B. Gatti and the frescoed bowl-shaped vault of the apse by M Anselmi.

a polychrome marble altar by *Domenico della Moschina*. The altar piece is also beautiful. It depicts the *Redeemer amongst a glory of Angels,* a work of 1605 by *Alessandro Mazzola.* In the large niche on the right, the bowl-shaped vault depicting the *Nativity of Christ worshipped by the shepherds* and the *Pentecost* and the large arch with the pictures of *Fortitude, Charity* and other feminine characters were realized between 1548 and 1567 by *Girolamo Mazzola Bedoli* with a magnificent scenic view received from *Parmigianino.* In the lateral chapel there's a beautiful monument *dedicated* to *Count Guido da Correggio*, realized in 1568 by *Giovan Battista Barbieri.*

The two altar pieces are marvellous: the first one, a work of 1605 by *Innocenzo Martini,* depicts *Madonna with Child between St. Hilary and St. John the Baptist;* the second one, a work of 1540 by *Simone delle Spade*, depicts the *Virgin on Throne with Child amongst the Saints Lucy, John the Baptist and musician Angels.* The marble altar was realized in 1775 by *Domenico della Meschina* on a design by *Antonio Brianti.*

Bernardino Gatti carried out the frescoes on the dome between 1560 and 1570 depicting the *Assumption of the Virgin.*

Although inspired by *Correggio's* frescoes in the dome of the Cathedral, it also shows influences by Michelangelo.

Odoardo Panini and *Carlo Guerrieri* realized the pulpit towards the end of the 18th century.

We now reach the presbytery, which is preceded by the large arch painted between 1530 and 1539 by *Lorenzo Mazzola,* known as Parmigianino.

The right hand side depicts the *Sage Virgins,*

which are holding lighted lamps, while the left hand side portrays the *Foolish Virgins*, which are holding doused lamps. Beside the Sage Virgins, we find the monochrome figures of *Aaron and Eve*, while beside the Foolish Virgins there are *Moses and Adam.*

All the Virgins, depicted in a rhythmic stance, are holding vases chiselled with gold and silver on their heads, which contain flowers and fruits.

The background of the large arch is red, paused with frames enclosing rosettes made of gold-plated copper, while the two lateral fascias are decorated with gold on a blue background.

The high altar and the balustrades of the entrance to the presbytery were realized by *Domenico della Meschina* on designs respectively by *Maurizio Lottici* and *Antonio Brianti.*

The polychrome marble floor surrounding the altar and the columns beside it are a fine work by *Giovanni Trivelloni*. The fresco on the apsidal bowl-shaped vault depicting the *Coronation of the Virgin* was realized between 1540 and 1547 by *Michelangelo Anselmi*, while *Pietro Rubini* decorated the walls two centuries later. *Gaetano Banzi* carved and inlayed the choir and the chancels around 1760. In the left-hand side chapel there's another beautiful altar realized in 1775 by *Domenico della Meschina. Antonio Bresciani* painted the canvas depicting the *Crucifixion* in 1783. The monuments to *Sforzino Sforza* and the Duke *Ottavio Farnese* are also fine works of art. They were carried out respectively by *Gian Francesco D'Agrate* and *Gianbattista Fornari*. In the following large niche we find the fresco in the bowl-shaped vault depicting the *Descent of the Holy Ghost on the Virgin and the Apostles*, realized between 1546 and 1553 by *Gerolamo Mazzola Bedoli*. The same author decorated the large arch, portraying *Judith holding the head of Holofernes*. The *Noble Sacristy* displays large walnut wardrobes that were realized between 1665 and 1670 by the Milanese carvers *Giambattista Mascheroni* and *Carlo Rottini. Lorenzo Aili* executed the statues of *St. Dominick* and *St. Rose* made of gilded wood between 1677 and 1681. The Flemish *John Sons* painted the altarpiece

depicting the *Holy Family* in 1607. The wardrobes store precious sacred vestments and furniture dating back to the 17th and 18th centuries. In the cellar we find the Sepulchral Chapel, whose construction was ordered in 1823 by Marie Louise. It preserves the mortal remains of 14 members of the *Farnese* and *Bourbon* families.

l) CHURCH OF ST. ALEXANDER

The first foundation was a convent of Benedictine nuns and dates back to the 9th century. The Church - the only part left after the convent was demolished in 1821 to build the *Royal Theatre* - was already dedicated to *St. Alexander*. It was rebuilt in 1527 on a design by *Bernardino Zaccagni*, and in 1622 the inside was completely refurbished by *Giovan Battista Magnani*, who also designed the

1: Church of the Steccata
   The large arch by Parmigianino (detail)
2: Church of St. Alexander - The facade

beautiful altar made of polychrome marbles with the urn of *St. Alexander* and the bell tower. The Neo-classic facade was rebuilt in 1784 on a design by *Antonio Bettoli.* The inside, with a single nave and 12 columns, is one of the most significant examples of the Mannerism of Emilia thanks to the richness of both the pictorial and the sculptural decorations.

In 1625 *Michele Colonna* carried out the vaults, showing balconies from which musicians Angels and putti stretch out. He is also the author of the decorations on the main arch and on those of the four lateral chapels. The fresco on the dome, depicting *Jesus raising the Mother kneeling down,* was realized in 1627 by *Alessandro Tiarini*, who is also the author of the painting on the left wall of the presbytery depicting the *Martyrdom of S. Alexander.*

L) FORMER CHURCH OF S. ANDREW

The first foundation in Romanesque style dates back to the 12th century.

While the external part remained virtually intact, the inside was completely restructured in 1736 and in 1830.

The building is currently used as a seat for art exhibitions and other events.

M) UNIVERSITY MUSEUM OF NATURAL HISTORY

It accommodates a magnificent *zoological museum*, occupied for the most part by vertebrate animals and rare insects.

The prestigious African collections of *Bottego* and *Piola* are stored here, while other collections by other illustrious naturalists such as *Strobel, Andreas* and *Del Prato* illustrate the faunal evolution of the Parmesan province. The attached laboratory, which performs environmental research activities, stores several collections, especially of invertebrate animals. It was founded in 1764 and it was gradually enriched thanks to the passionate work of the above mentioned naturalists. In 1980 it was reordered and established as a museum. It is now an object of study for many school classes, which are supplied with complete didactic information by the researchers. The latter also operate as guides.

N) CHURCH OF ST. ROCCO

The first construction dates back to the 16th century, and it was a thanksgiving by the city to *St. Rocco*, the protector against the plague, because the fateful effects of the epidemic were irrelevant.

In 1582 construction was stopped due to financial problems, and was resumed only at the end of the century by the Jesuits, who completed it in 1598.

It was rebuilt and extended between 1737 and 1754 on a design by the Bolognese architect *Alfonso Torreggiani,* while works were guided by the Parmesan *Adalberto della Nave* who slightly modified the outside. The building is one of the most significant examples of the Baroque of Emilia, with relevant influences coming from the then new born Rococo.

Unfortunately the facade is suffocated by the building facing it, therefore it's impossible to admire to its fullest the harmony of the Ionic and composite decorations, surmounted by a pediment.

Antonio Bettoli built the bell tower in 1747. The inside seems almost a theatrical scene, thanks to the abundance of stuccoes, lacquering and gilding decorating capitals, cornices, the beautiful choirs and the pulpit, designed by *Torreggiani* itself. The various chapels accommodate paintings from the 17th to the 19th century.

The reproduction of the *Lourdes Cave* placed in the chapel on the right hand side of the presbytery is rather peculiar, while in the left one we find the funereal monument dedicated to *Giacinta Santeville,* died in 1652, by her husband.

Torreggiani designed also the sacristy, with its rococo decorations standing out on the severe carved wood shelves on the walls.

1: *Former Church of St. Andrew - The ancient facade*
2: *On the left the palaces of the University and the bell tower of ST. Rocco*
3: *Church of St. Rocco - The beautiful Baroque inside*

O) STUARD ART GALLERY

It's located in the premises of the *Congregation of S. Filippo Neri,* which inherited from *Giuseppe Stuard* his collection of paintings composed of over 200 works of notable artistic value. Among them, many pertain to the Tuscany school of the 14th and 15th century and were realized by artists such as *Bicci di Lorenzo, Paolo di Giovanni Fei, Bernardo Daddi, Pietro di Giovanni Ambrosi* and *Niccolò di Tommaso.* Particularly notable is a pen drawing attributed to *Parmigianino* depicting a greyhound. Other works are attributed to *Guercino, Canaletto, Felice Boselli, Bartolomeo Schedoni, Ilario Spolverini* and others.

1: Madonna on the Throne with Child - Maestro della misericordia
2: Portrait of Luigi Berri Giuseppe Baldrighi
3: The Worship by the Sheperds - Franceso Fontebasso

ITINERARY NO. 2
A) Convent of St. Paul, *Via M. Melloni* • B) Glauco Lombardi Museum, Palace of the *Riserva*, *Piazza della Pace* • C) Church of St. Lucy, *Via Cavour* • D) The Bishop's Residence, *Piazza del Duomo* • E) Baptistery, *Piazza del Duomo* • F) Cathedral, *Piazza del Duomo* • G) Church and Monastery of St. John the Baptist, *Piazzale S. Giovanni* • H) Oratory of the Conception, *Via del Prato*

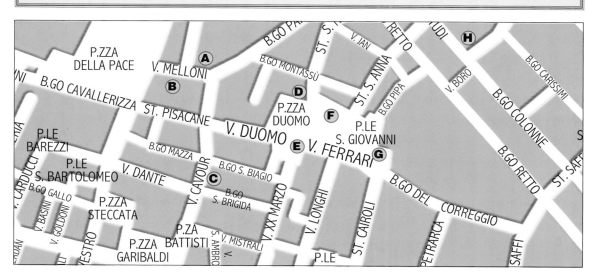

A) CONVENT OF ST. PAUL

The first foundation of the former convent dates back to the 10th century.

The Convent of the Benedictine Nuns dates back to the first years of the 11th century, but reached its maximum splendour between the end of 1400 and the beginning of 1500, when the Abbess was *Giovanna da Piacenza* who, among other things, commissioned *Correggio* and *Araldi* with the decoration of the rooms we will describe.

Correggio's Room

It's commonly referred to as *Room of St. Paul*, and was frescoed by *Correggio* _ a pupil of *Mantegna* _ in his younger years between 1518 and 1519, with a style inspired by the Renaissance.

Its plan is almost square, and the coat of arms of the *Abbess Giovanna* with three falcate moons is placed at the centre of the vault. 16 large vaulting ribs depart from the coat of arms, painted as bamboo canes, and enclose just as many gores decorated in pergola.

Under the gores there are figures of putti framed in ovals, under which lunettes contain mythological characters resting on the marble cornice.

West wall: the entrance to the room was moved from the east wall to the west wall, therefore we should start from the latter to visit this masterpiece. But we will start from the lunette, where the *God Pan* blows on a shell to strike *panic fear* into a maid's heart; she is *Integrity*, who nevertheless continues to fearlessly advance forward holding a dove, the symbol of purity (2nd lunette). In the 3rd lunette another maiden comes forward holding a lily, the symbol of *chastity*. These maidens represent Giovanna and her Nuns driving back the attacks of the authorities that wanted to resume the rule of enclosure.

In the oval above Pan one of the putti manages to deafen his companion that is stopping his ears. In the oval surmounting Integrity a putto is holding the head of a stag, the symbol of courage, and in the one surmounting chastity two putti are holding a garland of flowers, just the symbol of chastity.

19

North wall: the first lunette depicts *fortune*, while in the surmounting oval some putti seem to be climbing up a hill, symbolizing the ascent of the fortunate ones.

In the second lunette, *Bellona, Goddess of war and strife,* holds a spear and a torch, while the in the surmounting oval some putti are fighting for the possession of a sceptre.

In the third lunette the three Graces, the symbol of friendship, concord and peace, are surmounted in the oval by dancing putti.

In the fourth lunette, a young naked man with a garland on his head represent *Virtue,* and in the oval one of the putti tries to grasp the fruit festoons while another one is pointing at the sky.

In the centre of the wall the fireplace stands out. Its hood bears *Diana* on a carriage, with the forefront marked by a falcate moon similar to the one on the coat of arms of the Piacenza in the centre of the vault. In fact, Diana represents Abbess Giovanna looking just at the central rosette. Above Diana, the writing IGNEM GLADIO NE FODIAS (you will not poke the fire with the sword) is a reproof by Giovanna to the enemies that they should not try to obtain with force what she did not want to give them.

East wall: in this wall the four lunettes represent just as many natural elements.

In the first one, *water* is represented with a goddess called *Genius* representing welfare. There are some putti in the oval, one of whom is holding a sceptre with his right hand while holding a stone on his head with the left one; in the meantime a crown is being placed on his head by another putto. The crown with the sceptre symbolizes water as the *Queen of the elements.*

In the second lunette, *Tello,* a feminine goddess that has a cornucopia on her left arm while holding a big scorpion on her right hand, represents *Earth*. In the oval, two putti are fighting over a shield, the symbol of domination over the world. In the third lunette, *Air* is represented by *Juno* expiating the punishment described by Homer hanging in space, with two golden anvils under her feet; in the oval, a putto tries to hold a greyhound still. In the fourth lunette, *Fire* is represented by *Vesta* who had the task to maintain the eternal fire on; in the oval one of the putti extracts a fired arrow from the quiver.

1

2

South wall: the main theme of the lunettes relates to the *Goddesses,* and also includes the first one of the west wall that we hadn't described.

Saturn appears in the first one. In the oval, a putto holds a heavy spear pointing at Saturn, guilty of having deposed his father Uranus and devoured his sons, except for Jupiter.

The second lunette depicts the *Temple of Capitoline Jupiter,* while in the upper oval *two* putti are placing Jupiter's arrow in the bow.

In the third lunette the *three Parcae (Clotho, Lachesis* and *Atropos)* represent *fate,* to whom nobody can escape, while in the oval some putti are putting a lace on a rebelling dog, thus reinforcing the concept of the inevitability of destiny.

In the fourth lunette *Rhea Sylvia saves young Jupiter* while in the upper oval a putto looks sternly at Saturn because he would have liked to eat the son Jupiter too.

In the first lunette of the West wall the *Goddess Lucifer Diana,* symbolizing Giovanna da Piacenza, seems to welcome young Jupiter offering him the world, while in the oval one of the putti looks towards Diana and the other one looks in the opposite direction, which is to say towards Pan, while stopping his ears. As we have seen, the decoration has a mainly profane character, with many references to mythology; this makes it even stranger that is was ordered and commissioned by a Nun and executed in a Sacred building.

Leaving the Room of S. Paolo, we can admire two beautiful canvases in an adjacent room: the *Annunciation* and *The last Supper.* They wee painted between 1514 and 1516 by *Alessandro Araldi,* who also realized the frescoes decorating the nearby *Cell of St. Catherine.* Access to the latter room is possible from *Via P. Giordani.*

Room of Araldi: this room - which was part of Giovanna da Piacenza's private apartments like the one of S. Paolo - was frescoed by Araldi in 1514 in a late Gothic style, with an entanglement of grotesques enveloping ovals, bays and lunettes with sacred and profane subjects.

Correggio - Room of St. Paul
1: The north wall
2: The room of Araldi
3: The vault

Let's start the visit from the first double vaulting cell between the south and west walls, in which an Angel is trying to stop some winged horses from attacking some Sirens that are breast-feeding their sons.

South wall: in the first lunette a maiden breast-feeding the imprisoned father to save him symbolizes *Charity*. The second lunette depicts the *triumph of Emil Paul*, while the upper bay depicts *St. Paul falling from his horse*. In the third lunette, a maiden with a unicorn represents *Chastity*; in the bay, *Judith and Holofernes* confirm the belief of those times in the victory of chastity over lust.

West wall: in the three lunettes, mythological characters represent the theme of initiation to the truth under Giovanna's guide, placing one's own will under that of the Lord's representative.

North wall: Figures of dragons attacking putti and sirens represent the *temptation of the impossible* The same theme is depicted also in the lunettes, in the bays and on the hood of the fireplace.

East wall: Biblical characters represent the *victory of virtue over sin*, thanks to the submission to the Lord.

B) GLAUCO LOMBARDI MUSEUM

It's located in an enormous building built in the 16th century as quarters for the guest of the court, which is called *Palace of the riserva*. The court architect *Petitot* restored the part accommodating the museum in 1764. The rich collection of paintings, sculptures, furniture, furnishings and court dresses owes its existence to the passionate and tireless work of *Prof. Glauco Lombardi*. Over sixty years of the last century he tried to take back to Parma everything that had been created there, constituting as such a cultural richness. To achieve his goal he purchased many works even in antiquity markets. Therefore, we can enjoy a precious testimony of the arts, the customs and the garments of over a century of ducal life, spanning from the first half of the 18th century to the mid-19th. The collection particularly refers to *Marie Louise,* the wife of Napoleon and duchess of Parma, Piacenza and Guastalla from 1816 to 1847 century, beloved by her people and still now one of the noblest characters of the city. The visit begins from the *Great Hall*, decorated with many stuccoes, where a dress and a mantle

- enriched with platinum embroidering and wore by Marie Louise in official events - may be seen in the centre together with the *Corbeille* that Napoleon donated to Marie Louise in 1810 for their wedding. On the walls there is a large painting realized in 1812 by *R. Lefevre,* depicting Marie Louise as Empress of France, and other paintings. The showcases display jewels, objects and furnishings owned by the Duchess, Napoleon and their son, and a cast of the Duchess' hand by *Canova*. In the *Golden Hall we* can admire the original sketch of the Royal Theatre's curtain by *G. B. Borghesi,* and the *cup of the puerpera*. On the walls there are beautiful watercolour paintings by *G. Naudin* depicting the halls in the part of the Ducal Palace that was demolished to build the Royal Theatre. In the following hall dedicated to *Paolo Toschi,* the Director of the *Academy of Fine Arts,* there are many of his engravings. In the centre of the room there is a precious silk mantle donated to Marie Louise by the Chinese emperor *Kia King Kan*. On the walls there is a series of paintings by Parmesan artists of the 1800s. In the following *Hall of the Watercolours* we find a rich collection of paintings, watercolour paintings and engravings by Italian

and foreign artists of the 1700s and 1800s. The following *Hall of the French* accommodates Marie Louise's personal piano, with the original score of the opera *The Lombards to the First Crusade*, dedicated to the Duchess by *Giuseppe Verdi*. On the walls we find showcases containing personal belongings of Marie Louise, and paintings by Italian and French artists.

Continuing the visit one reaches the *Petitot Hall* where sketches, projects and engravings by the great architect are on display. The last room, dedicated to *Marie Louise,* displays other personal belongings of the Duchess and a marble bust of count *Neipperg,* Marie Louise's husband since 1821.

1: *The Palace of the Riserva, the seat of the G. Lombardi Museum*
2: *Marie Louise's platinum-embroidered dress*
3: *The corbeille Napoleon donated to Marie Louise*

C) CHURCH OF ST. LUCY

The first foundation dates back to 1220, but it owes its current appearance to a reconstruction performed at the end of the 17th century on a design by *Mauro Oddi.* The statues of *St. Hilary, St. Blaise* and *St. Lucy* stand out in the facade.

The latter Saint is depicted also in a marble medallion, a work of 1691 by *Giacomo Barbieri.* The inside has a single nave, with lateral chapels and a dome on the presbytery frescoed by *F. M. Galletti* with images of the Virgin, while the three spans of the nave depict scenes of St. Lucy's life. In the four lateral chapels there are paintings by various artists, while on the high altar there is a beautiful altarpiece depicting the *Communion of St. Lucy,* a work of 1730 by *Sebastiano Ricci.* Other fine works of art are the chancels, made of gilded and carved wood.

1: Church of St. Lucy - The facade
2: Via Cavour

D) THE BISHOP'S RESIDENCE

It's just in front of the Cathedral.

The first construction dates back to the first half of the 11th century, ordered by the *Bishop Count Cadalo*, the future anti-pope. It was completely rebuilt between 1172 and 1175 on commission by *Bishop Bernardo*.

Between 1232 and 1234 *Bishop Grazia* had the palace further extended, appointing the architect *Rolandello* as responsible for the works. The latter also the author of the porticoes and the three-light windows, still visible.

The internal portico was erected In the 15th century, during the bishopric of *Sagramoro*, while the external one was closed. Between 1553 and 1568 the palace was occupied by the *Duke Ottavio Farnese*, who is responsible for the beautiful coffered ceilings. In the 18th century, under *Bishop Camillo Marazzoni*, the palace underwent changes that modified its original appearance. The latter was recovered in this century with two restorations performed using the same materials as the original ones. The palace houses a rich collection of paintings depicting the Bishops that lived in it. Seven slabs dating back to the 12th century have been found in the Cathedral's Presbytery during the restoration and are also exhibited. On the ground there were four column-bearing

lions sculpted by *Benedetto Antelami* in 1178, now exhibited at the Diocesano Museum.

1: The internal courtyard
2: The facade

E) THE BAPTISTERY

The construction of this splendid irregular octagon-base monument began in 1196 on a design by the architect and sculptor *Benedetto Antelami,* who directed the works until 1216, when they were interrupted due to the lack of pink Veronese marble that covers the whole of the outside.

This was caused by the fights opposing Parma to Verona.

The works of the upper part began in 1259 and finished towards the end of the century. The Baptistery is one of the most important Italian medieval monuments; the style is Romanesque, but shows strong influences by the early French Gothic.

The building rests on a base with steps, and the eight facades have four rows of linteled small balconies surmounted by the last one that has blind pointed arches. On the roof, an elegant balustrade joins the eight slim lanterns placed on the corners.

There are three splayed portals, placed on the north (the one facing the square), west and south sides.

Moreover, the eight facades are decorated with 75 panels recalling the Ionic style, which contain the figures of fantastic and mythological animals.

North portal: Benedetto Antelami realized it. There are four elegant columns on the sides, supporting just as many decorations of the splayed arch and the architrave dividing the jambs from the upper lunette.

The left jamb bears the sculpture of the *Genealogy of Jesus Christ* enclosed between the figures of *Jacob,* below, and *Moses,* on top; the right one depicts the *Genealogy of the Virgin Mary.*

In the architrave biblical scenes depicting *Jesus baptized by the Baptist,* the *Banquet of Herod* and *Salome and the beheading of the Baptist* surmount Latin writings referring to Benedetto Antelami and the year works began (1196). The lunette is framed by a sculptured frieze portraying the *twelve Apostles,* and depicts a *Virgin with Child* between the Magi, on the left, and an Angel advising St. Joseph to escape to Egypt, on the right. On the upper sides of the arch there are two beautiful sculptures of the *Archangels Gabriel and Michael.*

West portal: this is also a work by Antelami, and has on each side four slim columns sup-

porting the friezes of the arch and the architrave, just like the north one. In the left jamb there is the sculpture of the six works of *Mercy leading to Redemption,* while in the left one the same theme is depicted with the *Parable of the vineyard.*

Two angels playing the *Horns for the resurrection of the dead* are depicted in the centre of the architrave; on the left, the Elected ones are rejoicing, while on the right the contrite Wicked ones cover their bodies.

In the centre of the lunette we can admire a large figure of the *Redeemer on Throne* showing the wounds on his hands, amongst Angels with the instruments of the Passion surrounded by an arched lintel with the sculpture of the *twelve Apostles,* just like the one of the north portal, but this time divided on top by two angels.

It's the first Italian sculpture depicting the *Last Judgement.*

South portal: it's the least decorated of the three, and probably realized after the other two by Antelami's pupils.

As opposed to the other two, it only has three columns on its two sides. Jambs are not sculptured, while the architrave bears three medallions: *Christ* in the centre, the *Baptist* and the *Agnus Dei* on the two sides.

The lunette encircled by a frieze with floral motives, presents scenes taken from the Eastern novel *Barlaam and Josafat.*

A masculine figure (*mankind*) high on the tree of life, whose base is gnawed by two mice, collects honey (*the sweetness of life*) from a beehive, while a dragon (*the devil*) threatens him with flames. *Apollo* on the left in a double portrait of the sun and *Diana,* the moon, on the right, represent the endless succession of days and nights.

Inside: it's subdivided into 16 sides that rise up towards as many sections of the dome separated by pink marble vaulting ribs. At ground level each side has a niche surmounted by two elegant small balconies of the *matroneo.* The extremely elegant whole

1: The Baptistery seen from the Cathedral
2: Northern Portal
3: Western Portal
4: Southern Portal

is mainly characterized by the Gothic Style. Let's start the visit of the 16 niches by entering from the north portal facing the square. In the lunette surmounting the portal, considered as the first niche, we can admire the *Escape to Egypt*, a high relief executed by the pupils of Antelami that recalls the theme of the external lunette. The upper fresco portrays two Saints. Turning on the right, we reach the **2nd niche:** in the lunette the Archangel St. Michael between two Saints tramples upon two dragons. In the upper fresco, attributed to the Tuscan painter *Buffalmacco*, St. George pierces the dragon.

3rd niche: the lunette portrays the *Annunciation of the Virgin*. The upper fresco is subdivided in bays depicting the Passion of Christ and figures of Saints.

4th niche: the lunette portrays the *Archangel Gabriel*. The upper fresco, once again subdivided in bays, portrays other scenes of the Passion.

5th niche: (West portal): this lunette, by Antelami, also refers to the external one (The Last Judgement).

In fact the figure of *King David,* a symbol of Christ, appears in the centre while playing the decahedron, sided by dancers and musi-

Baptistery
1: *Southern internal lunette - B. Antelami*
   La presentazione al tempio
2: *The Semidome of Northeast niche*
3: *Wonderful indoors; the Font*
   in the foreground

cians (*The Kingdom of the Just*). The upper fresco depicts two saints.

6th niche: the lunette shows the Archangel Gabriel between two Saints. The upper fresco portrays the *Virgin on throne* amongst various Saints.

7th niche: in the lunette, the Archangel Gabriel is once again between two saints blessing children. The upper fresco is subdivided in four bays: the *Resurrection*, the *Baptism of Christ,* the *Baptism of Constantine* and the *Wedding of St. Catherine.*

8th niche: the lunette depicts *S. Francesco of Assisi*, a Seraph with six wings and a character of the Apocalypse. The upper fresco shows the *Birth of Jesus Christ*, above, and below 6 bays with figures of Saints.

9th niche (south portal): it's a work by Antelami.

The lunette portrays the *Circumcision*, which recalls the theme of the external lunette (*The tree of life*).

10th niche: the upper lunette portrays *The Redeemer,* above, and below figures of Evangelists and Apostles. In the upper fresco, above, the Virgin breast-feeds Jesus amongst Saints; below, the Baptist in the desert and other Saints.

11th niche: in the lunette the *Redeemer* blesses the Archangel Gabriel from above, while the latter is piercing a dragon amongst Evangelists and Saints. The upper fresco depicts the *Virgin with Child on the Throne between two Saints.*

12th niche: in the lunette an Angel is sided by *St. Ambrose* and *St. Jerome*. The fresco portrays *Christ on the Cross* with the Virgin and Saints, above; below, *Our Lady of Mercy* between two saints.

13th niche: it's placed behind the high altar, eastward, according to what the orientation of the times was.

In the centre of the lunette we find *Christ in Glory* amongst Saints and symbolic animals. The upper part of the fresco shows *the Baptism of Jesus;* below, we can see *The Virgin with Child* amongst angels.

14th niche: in the lunette, *Jesus Christ* overlooks an Angel and four characters. In the upper part of the fresco God and the Holy Ghost are blessing the Coronation of the Virgin by Jesus; below, figures of Saints, of the King of France, St. Louis, Our Lady and St. Michael.

15th niche: St. Agatha

16th niche: the lunette depicts an Angel between two Saints. The fresco portrays *The Virgin on Throne with Child* between the Archangel Gabriel, on the left, and the Baptist introducing Cardinal Gherardo Bianchi, on the right.

It's the first Emilian portrait that is influenced by Giotto.

As we have seen, only two lunettes, the 5th and 9th, are works by Antelami, while the others are by his pupils.

Among the frescoes only the one of the 13th niche dates back to the 13th century, while

all the others are from the 14th.

In the centre we can admire the large *Baptismal Font,* excavated in 1299.

On the right hand side of the south portal a small *aspersion font* rests on a lion holding a hare in his claws.

On the corners of the niches it's possible to enjoy the statues of the *months* and *seasons*, which are believed to have been realized personally by *Antelami*, or in any case under his direct supervision because they reveal a unique execution.

The visit starts with March, which was then the first month of the year.

March: plays the flute

April: it's the King of months, therefore it's crowned.

May: it's a horseman holding a sickle. June: it's a man reaping wheat. July: it's a man threshing with horses. August: it's a man repairing a cask. September: it's a man harvesting grapes. October: it's a man sawing. November: it's a man harvesting vegetables. December: it's a man gathering wood. January: it's a two-faced man, like Janus, warming himself by the fire. February: It's a man spading the ground.

Some statues show the zodiacal signs, while the missing ones are walled in the first gallery.

Winter: it's a half-naked man carrying a branch on the bare shoulder to recall the passage from the mild to the cold season.

Spring: it's an elegantly dressed sweet femi-nine figure with a garland of flowers on her head.

It's one of the finest works of the cycle, and mirrors the passage from Romanesque to Gothic.

There is no news of the other two seasons.

The dome: as we have mentioned above, it's subdivided vertically in 16 gores and horizontally in 5 fascias included between the red sky surrounding the keystone and the pointed arches (eight of which with a window) resting on the architrave of the second floor of the women's gallery.

1st fascia: it has an azure background with lozenges, each of which containing a star.

2nd fascia: it depicts the twelve Apostles and the four Evangelists.

3rd fascia: the gore above the altar bears *Christ on throne* between *Our Lady* on the left and the *Baptist* on the right.

In the remaining thirteen sections there are as many *Prophets*.

4th fascia: it depicts twelve episodes of the life of the Baptist, and four Saints.

5th fascia, (the arches): it presents episodes of *Abraham*'s life, the four natural elements (*water, air, fire* and *earth*), the four seasons and the *Virgins*.

Baptistery
1: Main Font
2: Small Font
3: Sheba's Queen and King Solomon
4: Dome

3

4

1: Façade and bell tower
2: Cathedral's planimetry
3: Nave

F) THE CATHEDRAL

Although modified in the following centuries, the Cathedral remains one of the most notable examples of the Romanesque Art of the Po Valley. Its construction began in the second half of the 11th century. It was consecrated in 1106 and dedicated to St. *Mary of the Assumption.* Like the Baptistery, the Cathedral was designed by *Benedetto Antelami.* These two splendid monuments one by the other make *Piazza Duomo* one of the finest Italian squares.

An earthquake in 1117 caused severe damages, thus the works were finished only in 1130. Modifications to the covering were carried out between 1160 and 1170. In the second half of the 13th century the upper part of the facade was changed, covering with Veronese pink marble the small balcony and the upper cornice, while the rest of the facade remained of sandstone.

The facade: there are three rows of small balconies with round arches supported by elegant small columns; two are horizontal while the upper one follows the slopes of the roof.

Of the three wooden portals realized in

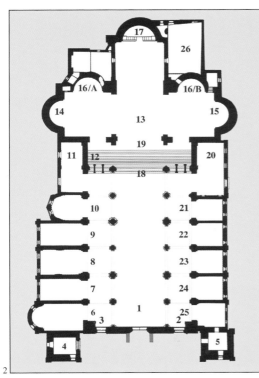

1) Nave
2) Right aisle
3) Left aisle
4) Small tower
5) Long tower
6) Chapel of the Consorziali
7) Chapel of the Crucifix
8) Chapel of the Blessed Sacrament
9) Chapel Annunziata
10) Chapel Valeri
11) Chapel of Saint Theresa
12) Chapel of Saint Severus
13) Correggio's Dome
14) Chapel of Assunta
15) Chapel Montini
16/A) Chapel of Saint Fermo
16/B) Chapel of Saint Paolo
17) Central apses
18) Great staircase
19) Crypt
20) Chapel of Saint Agatha
21) Chapel Centoni
22) Chapel of the Town or Chapel of the Saints Sebastian and Fabian
23) Chapel Baiardi, former Chapel Lalatta
24) Chapel Cantelli
25) Chapel Bernieri, former Chapel Ardemani
26) Consorziali's Sacristy

1494 by *Luchino Bianchino*, the central one is preceded by an arch supported by two columns resting on columniferous lions, and is surmounted by an elegant small balcony. The arch was realized in 1281 by *Giambono da Bissone*, who used an older one depicting the months symbolized by characters performing agricultural works.

The square-base bell tower rises on the right hand side. The square-base bell tower rises on the right hand side. It was built between 1284 and 1291, and is 63 metres high. There's a gilded copper copy of an angel on the summit. The original one is inside the Diocesano Museum. The upper part has an elegant three-light window on each side; on top, there's an elegant column balustrade with four spandrels on the corners.

On the left there's a tower that remained incomplete, built in 1602 by the architect *Smeraldo Smeraldi*.

3

The outside: the large area of the apses, the transepts and the choir is crossed horizontally by a fascia of coffers, just like the Baptistery, on which mythological and fantastic animals are sculptured.

The lower arches are blind, while the ones of upper part and the octagonal dome are round and supported by slim small columns. The capitals of the pilasters of the lower arches bear biblical and apocalyptic characters.

The sacristies and the sides accommodating the lateral chapels were added between the 13th and 14th century.

The inside: it has the shape of a Latin cross and is subdivided in three naves separated by large columns that also support the women's gallery, the latter beautified by elegant three-light windows.

The presbytery and the transepts are very high, in order to allow space for the underlying cellar.

Central nave: the counter-facade bears on the sides of the central portal the portraits of *Lattanzio Gambara* and *Bernardino Gatti*, who frescoed the surmounting *Ascension* between 1571 and 1573. In the centre of the wall the recent stained-glass large window portrays *St. Bernard,* St. *Hilary* and *the Sacred Mount.* The large frescoes depicting *Scenes from the life of Jesus* surmounting the women's gallery are works by the same authors. The Baroque holy water stoups and pulpit date back to the second half of the 16th century. The capitals of the pilasters dividing the three naves and those of the women's galleries were realized in Romanesque style by Lombard workers in the first half of the 12th century. They depict the theme of the *fight between good and evil* with biblical and fantastic scenes, episodes of medieval life and figures of saints. Some of the capitals bear bent acanthus leaves and interlacing branches,

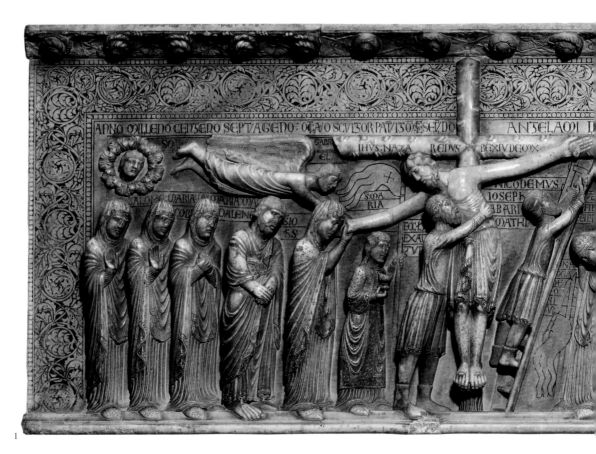

1

recalling the Corinthian style. The cross-vault, with transepts crossing in the centre and forming large carved wood rosettes, was frescoed between 1555 and 1557 by *Gerolamo Mazzola Bedoli* and *Francesco Mendogni* with head and shoulder portraits of Prophets and vegetal decorations.

Right nave: above the portal it's possible to admire *The Visitation*, a fresco realized in 1575 by *Alessandro Mazzola Bedoli*.

Alessandro Mazzola Bedoli frescoed the vaults of the whole nave between 1572 and 1573 with *putti playing amongst flowers*.

1st Chapel: it accommodates the tombs of the *Ardemani* and *Bernieri* family members, who died in the 15th century.

Two telamons dating back to the 12th century are inserted in the recently rebuilt altar. Above the altar, there is a beautiful canvas depicting the *Visitation of Mary to St. Elizabeth*. It's a work of the first years of '500 by *Cristoforo Caselli*.

2nd Chapel: it's dedicated to the *Cantelli* family. *Girolamo Magnani* realized the frescoes on the vault and the walls in 1881.

3rd Chapel: it's called *Bajardi*, and it's dedicated to the fallen soldiers of the First World War. *Biagio Biagetti*, the director of the National Art Gallery, realized the frescoes in 1922.

4th Chapel: it's known as *Chapel of the Commune* because the municipal Coat of arms appears repeatedly on the frescoes on the vault and the walls. The frescoes were painted in the first half of the 15th century and depict *scenes from the life and the miracles of the Sts. Sebastian and Fabian*. The black-and-white marble niche encloses a beautiful altarpiece realized in 1526 by *Michelangelo Anselmi* depicting *Madonna with Child amongst the Saints Blaise, Hilary, Rocco and Sebastian*.

5th Chapel: it's dedicated to the Centoni family, and a 15th-century sarcophagus con-

Cathedral
1: Upper right transept
  Benedetto Antelami - The deposition (1178)
2: The high altar

35

tains the mortal remains of Ludovico, an illustrious jurist of the times.

The wrought-iron gate dates back to the 15th century.

The frescoes on the walls were realized in 1530 by *Francesco Maria Rondani* and depict in the upper part *episodes of the Passion of Christ,* and in the lower one *Scenes from the life of St. Antonio Abate. Andrea Pezzali* painted the frescoes on the vault in the 18th century. Above the altar a large canvas realized in 1516 by *Alessandro Araldi* portrays a *Madonna with Child and the Sts. Paul and Antonio Abate.* The altar-facing depicting *St. Antonio Abate and St. Catherine* is by the same author.

6th Chapel: it's dedicated to *St. Agatha,* and may be entered by crossing an 18th-century wrought iron gate.

Sebastiano Galeotti realized the frescoes on the vault in 1719.

Above the altar a beautiful and finely decorated marble niche encloses a canvas painted between 1566 and 1574 by *Bernardino Gatti,* which portrays *Jesus on the Cross and Magdalene, St. Agatha and St. Bernard at his feet.*

Upper right transept: it may be reached by going up a few steps and crossing a beautiful marble balustrade by *Gerolamo Mazzola Bedoli.*

A masterpiece by *Benedetto Antelami* is walled in the right wall. The author signed it and dated it 1178 with a Latin phrase. It's the high relief portraying *the Deposition,* realized in Romanesque style although the French Gothic influence is strong. In the centre *Jesus* is being deposed from the cross by *Joseph of Antinea* supporting him on the left, while on the right *Nicodemus* on the ladder is about to remove the nail in his left hand.

Starting from the left hand side we see the *Three Mary's, St. John the Evangelist,* The *Virgin* caressing the right hand of the Son already detached from the cross, and then a smaller figure holding a chalice in the right hand and a ensign on the left one, which represents the *Triumph of the Church.* On the right of the cross, after Nicodemus, a feminine character with a broken ensign represents the *defeat of the Synagogue;* a centurion and another five characters follow. In front of the latter, on the fore-

ground, Roman soldiers are staking Jesus' robes on dices.

The characters on the left are surmounted by the *Archangel Gabriel* holding out Jesus' hand to Our Lady, while on the right the *Archangel Raphael* bows the Synagogue's head. Th whole of the characters we have just described is enclosed above and on the sides by a finely chiselled frame. On the upper corners two garlands enclose the faces of the *Sun*, on the left, and the *Moon*, on the right. According to some studies, this slab and the four lions placed on the sides of the internal part of the portal, a slab that is now almost destroyed, the two telamons inserted in the altar of the first chapel on the right and three capitals now stored in the *National Gallery* were all part of a pulpit placed in the presbytery. On the same wall it's possible to admire two large canvases realized in the 16th century by *Ercole Procaccini* portraying *King David and St. Cecilia*.

Cathedral
1: The central nave seen from the presbytery
2: The dome by Correggio
Page 38-39 - The Cathedral and the Baptistery seen from the Bishop's residence.

2

Capitular archive: it may be accessed by going up a wooden staircase. Beautiful illuminated codices and manuscripts are on display.

Montini Chapel: the frescoes on the apse with the Lord's bust amongst arabesques were realized between 1505 and 1507 by *Cristoforo Caselli.* The same artist is the author of the pictorial part of the tomb of the *Canon Bartolomeo Montini,* while the sculptural part was carried out by *Gian Francesco D'Agrate.*

Michelangelo Anselmi realized the first frescoes on the vault in 1548, but later on they were ruined by humidity. In 1768 *Antonio Bresciani* redid them.

Chapel of St. Paul: *Pomponio Allegri,* the son of *Correggio,* frescoed the apse between 1560 and 1562.

Above the altar there's a fine altarpiece portraying *The Conversion of St, Paul* painted by *Antonio Bresciani* in 1796.

Sacristy of the *Consorziali*: it may be reached through a door on the right of the choir. The benches, the wardrobes and the large central case-rack are real masterpieces of the carving and inlaying art. *Cristoforo da Lendinara* began the works in 1488, and *Luchino Bianchino*, the author of all the framing, finished them in 1495. Inlays are realized following a precise perspective, an evident result of the co-operation between Lendinara and *Piero della Francesca.* Lendinara received his son Bernardino's help to carry out the large case rack.

Presbytery: the 17th-century altar is on the centre. A white and pink marble ark dating back to the 12th century was inserted in it. On the left-hand side, we find a *Blessing Christ* and the symbols of the four Evangelists, and on the right hand side the *Saints Abdom* and *Sennen amongst the lions.* The centre portrays the martyrdom of the two saints, and on the sides we can see the figures of nine Apostles.

The cross and the candelabrums on the altar, the two marble tribunes placed on the sides, and the two statues portraying *St. Benedict*, on the left, and *St. Scholastica*, on the right, all date back to the 16th-17th century.

The dome: it's one of *Correggio's* masterpieces. He erected it between 1526 and 1530 during the works he had been entrusted with by the *Councilmen of the Cathedral* with the innovative spirit aroused by the Renaissance. *Correggio* had the eight large circular windows in the tambour opened in order to give more light to the dome, and had the four large pendentives on the corners modelled in the shape of a shell. The subject of the fresco is the *Assumption of the Virgin into Heaven.* The ascension occurs amid a jubilation of Angels, which push the Virgin preceded by an Angel (Gabriel) towards Heaven, while singing, playing music and embracing one another. At the base of the dome the Apostles look at the triumph of the miraculous Assumption in ecstasy, overlooked by children burning incense. The quality with which the elements forming the whole are assembled is splendid, and the ascending movement towards the Empyrean is rendered faultlessly in the heavenly mistiness of the sky. The four shells depict the four

protectors of Parma. Starting from right and moving counter clockwise we find: *St. Hilary*, with a large yellow cloak; *St. Thomas* with a large red cloak; *St. John the Baptist* with the lamb; *St Bernard* with an Angel holding his pastoral. *Gerolamo Mazzola Bedoli* realized the rest of the presbytery area, including the arch, because *Correggio* had left the works due to quarrels with the commissioners. Probably they did not understand his innovative style that spanned from the majesty of Renaissance to the refinement of Baroque.

The choir: *Cristoforo Da Lendinara* carved and inlayed the stalls between 1469 and 1473. Only 22 were foreseen but there are now 40, and it is still to be determined whether the additional ones were made by Cristoforo himself, by the son *Bernardino* or by *Luchino Bianchino*.

Gerolamo Mazzola Bedoli frescoed the vault in 1530 with floral motives.

Bishop's chair: it may be reached from the choir by going up a staircase.

Benedetto Antelami executed this marble

work between 1187 and 1196. It's a throne resting on two seated dogs, while on the sides there are the sculptures of *St. George killing the dragon,* on the left, and *The conversion of St. Paul*, on the right. The two lion-shaped armrests are supported by two telamons. Above the chair, a large niche contains a beautiful marble ciborium realized between 1486 and 1490 by *Alberto Maffeolo da Carrara.*

Gerolamo Mazzola Bedoli frescoed the bowl-shaped vault between 1538 and 1544, portraying the *Last Judgement.*

Upper left transept

Chapel of St. Fermo: the altar, the niche and the ark of *St. Fermo*, all made of marble, were done in the 18th century, while the vault, depicting *Moses advising people to escape from a serpent,* the symbol of the devil, was frescoed two century earlier by *Orazio Sarnacchini,* who also frescoed the whole cross-vault of the transept.

The crypt of the Cathedral

Chapel of Our Lady of the Assumption: the beautiful altarpiece above the altar was realized by *Giovan Battista Tinti* in 1589 and depicts the *Assumption of the Virgin.*

On the left wall two large canvases painted in 1560 by *G. C. Procaccini* depict some warriors. *Orazio Sarnacchini* frescoed the vault of the apse in 1575, portraying *Moses getting water to spring from the rocks.* Going down the staircase leading to the lower left transept one may enjoy a large canvas depicting a *Crucifix with the Franciscan Saints,* which was painted in 1753 by *Gaspare Traversi.*

Chapel of St. Theresa: on the altar there's a beautiful sculpture of *St. Theresa in ecstasy.* Another fine work of art is the large canvas portraying *St. Bernardino Praying*, a work by *Sandrino Badalocchio.*

Crypt: as we have already mentioned before, it's located under the presbytery and the two transepts, and may be accessed by crossing a beautiful wrought-iron gate dating back to the 15th century. The columns of the atrium date back to the 11th century, and the capitals bear acanthus leaves.

Turning on the right we find the **chapel of**

St. Bernardino: it accommodates the sepulchre of St. *Bernard.*

Above the ark, there's the statue of the Saint with two Angels on the sides, a work by *Prospero Spani.* The frescoes on the vault and on the four lunettes describe episodes of the Saint's life.

Chapel of St. Agapito: the polychrome marble niche of the altar encloses the statue of the Saint, which was sculptured in the 16th century by *Gianbattista Barbieri.* The 15th-century low relief depicting the *Blessed Simona Cantulli* is a fine work of art.

Rusconi chapel: it was built in the first years of the 16th century, and the Bishop of Parma, *Giovanni Rusconi,* dedicated it to *St. John.* The portrait of the Bishop kneeling down *appears* on the right in a canvas depicting the *Virgin on Throne between the Saints John the Evangelist and John the Baptist.*

On the walls there are busts of Prophets, Patriarchs, Saints and Kings, enclosed in niches. The frescoes decorating the walls and the vault are beautiful. They date back to the 15th century and are painted in Lombard Gothic style, with influences from the Venetian School.

In the centre, a beautiful sculptural group depicts *The Madonna with Child between St. Joseph and another Saint.*

Central chapel: two *Roman mosaics* dating back to the 4th century AD are inserted in the floor. They were found in the square in front of the Cathedral during the excavation works carried out in 1955.

The altar is dedicated to *St. Hilary* and is surmounted by a beautiful canvas depicting the Saint, painted in 1733 by *Antonio Balestra.*

Ravacaldi chapel: the *Canon Antonio Ravacaldi* had it built in the first half of the 15th century. The walls are frescoed with *Scenes from the Virgin's life*: *The Nativity* on the right wall, *The Annunciation* on the bottom wall, *The Marriage; The presentation of Mary to the Temple.*

The scenes of the various frescoes, realized in French Gothic style, follow one another with narrative continuity and form a very pleasant whole.

₂

The author is unknown, but recent studies attribute them to *Bartolino de'Grossi*. The vaults portray *Christ Pantocrator* and floral motifs.

Left chapel: on the altar there is a beautiful canvas painted in 1520 by *Alessandro Araldi* portraying *The Wedding of the Virgin*. The wooden choir carved in 1555 by *Matteo Fabi is* a fine work of art.

Chapel of St. Agnes: a fresco painted in 1526 by *Michelangelo Anselmi* depicts the *Virgin appearing to her family*.

The Cathedral
1: Crypt - 4th-5th cent. mosaic
2: The frescoes in the Valeri chapel, the 5th one of the left nave.

Left nave

5th chapel: the *Valeri* family had it built. It is wholly covered with Gothic style frescoes, both on the walls and the vaults, which were painted in the first half of the 15th century by *Bartolino de' Grossi.* The base is octagonal, and slim columns divide the walls that portray *Scenes from the lives of the Saints Andrew the Apostle, Catherine and Christopher* divided in bays. All the scenes depict many characters moving in small environments. The style is Lombard Gothic, with a spirit of raw realism that describes the scenes from *The Martyrdom of the Saints* in their full brutality.

The vault sections, separated by vaulting ribs that are an extension of the columns, narrate in golden round frames on blue background eight *Stories from the life of Mary and the birth of Christ.*

The gilded wood altar is a work by *Ignazio Marchetti* dating back to the 1700s. A niche on the right portrays a *dead Christ,* a work by an unknown artist of the 15th century.

4th chapel: the two portraits of the *Madonna of the Angels* are fine works of art. The first one is a 16th-century canvas inserted in the yellow and black marble niche above the altar, while the second one is a white marble statue of the 17th century.

3rd chapel: the altar-facing encloses a 19th-century canvas depicting *The dinner of Jesus in Emmaus.*

The two statues depicting *Faith and Fortitude* are also from the 19th century.

2nd chapel: *Gaspare Fatuli* built it in 1488. *Gaspare Traversi* carried out the four paintings on the wall in 1753. They depict *The Saints Lucy, Agatha and Apollonia; Saint Antonio da Padova; St. Peter; Saints adoring the Eucharist.*

1st chapel: a canvas by *Francesco Monti* depicting *The Visitation* surmounts the altar. A 16th-century statue portraying *Francesco Carpesano* is a fine work of art.

The fresco of the entrance pilaster painted in 1496 by *Alessandro Araldi* portrays a *Madonna with Child*, and is another splendid work of art.

The Cathedral
1: The magnificent portal
2: The right side
3: Church of St. John the Evangelist.
*   Facade and bell tower.*

G) CHURCH AND MONASTERY OF ST. JOHN THE EVANGELIST.

The first foundation of the Romanesque-style Benedictine complex dated back to the 10th century but was destroyed by a fire towards the end of the 15th century. Its reconstruction was decided in Renaissance style, and was carried out between 1490 and 1519 under the guidance of *Giliolo da Reggio* first and then under that of *Bernardino Zaccagni,* elongating the apsidal part.

The project was followed and continuously updated by the Benedictine monks, which created here an important cultural centre attended by all the intellectuals of the city.

But the facade was left uncompleted, and the completion began in 1604 under the direction of the Ducal architect *Simone Moschino*, following the dictates of the rising Baroque style.

The facade: it was carried out in three years by *Giambattista Carrà da Bissone*, who is also the author of the seven statues decorating it. The lower part has three portals: the central one is sided and surmounted by three statues in niches, while the lateral ones are surmounted by large glass rosettes.

The upper part has a large stained-glass window in the centre, sided by two statues; another two statues are on the sides, supported by decorated pilasters.

A large copper rosette stands out above a second architrave, in which a royal eagle - the symbol of the Baptist - is inserted.

The square-base bell tower with an octagonal belfry was built starting from 1618 on a design by *G. Battista Magnani*.

The inside: it has the shape of a Latin cross, with three naves divided by arcades and supported by cross-shaped pilasters with capitals surmounted by dices.

The style is that of the Renaissance.

The vaults of the three naves, of the transepts and of the presbytery are of the cross type.

The wall on the counter-facade bears a large painting portraying the *Vision of St. John in the isle of Patmos*, painted in 1687 by *Giovanni Battista Merano*.

The two white-marble holy water stoups placed in line with the two first columns are fine works of art.

Central nave: the arches and the cross-vaults were frescoed around 1520 by *Michelangelo Anselmi* depicting putti, chandeliers and symbols of St. John.

The grotesques painted on the semi-pilasters and the frieze running along the two walls continuing the one already executed by others in the right transept are instead by *Correggio*, who painted them between 1522 and 1523 continuing its theme, inspired by sacrifice.

The monochrome frieze is interrupted by scenes depicting *The sacrifice of the Lamb* and *the Altar of the unknown God.*

Devotion and sacrifice also inspire the other scenes. On the sides of the scenes, *Prophets* are holding Latin writings and *Sibyls* are holding Greek writings, all concerning the life of Christ. Each one of the two lateral naves has six polygon-base chapels.

Right nave

First chapel:

It's dedicated to the *Archangel Michael* who appears in a painting placed in a gilded-wood niche, *sided by St. Jerome at the feet of Our Lady.*

The frescoes on the walls have decorative elements, while in one on the ceiling depicts the Archangel beside the Eternal Father.

Tommaso Aldovrandini and *Antonio Boni* painted them in the first years of 1700.
The funereal monument dedicated to *Alberico Sanvitale* is also beautiful.
Second chapel: it's dedicated to *St. Antonio*. Above the altar, there's a fine canvas depicting *the Nativity*, painted in 1519 by the Bolognese brothers *Giacomo* and *Giulio Francia*.
The frescoes on the walls were painted in the first years of 1700 by Aldovrandini and Boni, and depict musician Angels on a balcony, while the apse bears the *Assumption*.
Third chapel: it's dedicated to St. *Felicity*.
In the centre a fine canvas painted in 1499 by *Cristoforo Caselli* portrays the *Worship of the Magi* with an almost miniated technique.
The frescoes on the wall, by Boni, depict *The Martyrdom of some Saint women*.
Fourth chapel: it's dedicated to *St. James*.
Above the altar, a beautiful altarpiece painted by *Gerolamo Bedoli Mazzola* in 1542 portrays a *Madonna with child and St. James*.
The frescoes on the walls and the vault, carried out in 1684 by *Giovan Battista Merano*, depict episodes of the life, the Martyrdom and the Glory of St. James.
Fifth chapel: it's dedicated to the *Del Bono* family, who commissioned two large canvases to *Correggio: The Deposition* and *The martyrdom of four Saints*. The canvases we now see on the walls are copies executed in the 18th century, while the originals can be admired in the *National Gallery*.
The drawings under the arch are certainly by Correggio, while the attribution of the frescoes depicting *God between the Sts. Peter and Andrew*, on the right, and *The fall of St, Paul*, on the left, is uncertain.
The Bolognese *Michele Colonna* and *Giacomo Alboresi* painted the frescoes on the walls and the vault between 1667 and 1672.
Sixth chapel: on the altar, a beautiful altarpiece depicts *St. Frances Romana*, while the frescoes painted by *Colonna* and *Alboresi* portray *Angels with lily and sword flying in the sky*.
Right transept: a blue monochrome frieze runs on it horizontally, with scenes of Sacrifices alternated with round frames enclosing busts of Saints, Popes and Prophets. The

fresco is attributed to *Alessandro Araldi*.
On the right, in a niche, two fine statues of *St. Felicity and the son Vitalis*, and *St. Benedict;* they are made of whitened terracotta, and were carried out in 1543 by the *Antonio Begarelli*, from Modena.
Chapel of St. John: he was the first abbot of the monastery, and his mortal remains are preserved in the urn under the altar. The apsidal bowl-shaped vault is frescoed with episodes of his life that were painted in 1520 by *Michelangelo Anselmi*.
The baroque niche above the altar encloses the altarpiece portraying *The miracle of St. John Abbot*, a work painted in 1674 by the Bolognese *Emilio Taruffi*.
Chapel of St. Scholastica: it's located on the right of the high altar. The arch is frescoed beautifully with a portrait by *Alessandro Mazzola Bedoli* depicting St. *Cecilia sitting at the organ and St. Margaret*.
On the sides there are two canvases: *Madonna with child and two Bishops* by *Rondani*, and *Madonna with Child and Saints* attributed to *Anselmi's* pupils.
Behind the altar a painting by an unknown artist of the 17th century depicts *The death of St. Scholastica*.
The dome: it's placed between the two transepts. To admire it in the best possible perspective it's better to move to the limit of the steps of the presbytery.
In realizing this 1520 masterpiece -therefore before frescoing the dome of the Cathedral with which he reached the apotheosis - *Correggio* used once again the technique of ascending movement, giving the onlooker the impression of really watching an open sky. The whole has lesser characters when compared with the dome of the Cathedral, and *Christ* dominates the centre of the scene in a golden sky. He almost seems to descend from it to summon *St. John the Evangelist*, placed beneath under a circle of clouds on which the *Apostles* and some putti are resting.

Church of St. John the Evangelist
The central nave

The setting has been interpreted in several ways. The assumption that it is the Ascension of the Redeemer is contrasted by the fact that His mantle flutters upwards, proving a descending movement rather than an ascending one.

It was then interpreted as the *Vision of St. John in the isle of Patmos*, but more recent studies confirmed it as *The transit of St. John*, depicted in his elder years while leaving the underlying world to be reached by Jesus and ascend to Heaven with him.

The majesty of the whole and the Renaissance characters recall the Michelangelesque style of the *Sistine Chapel*, but *Correggio* adds his personal innovative touch that anticipates the following Baroque style.

Correggio frescoed the pendentives and the under-arches depicting *Biblical scenes* and *the Fathers of the Church* in the immediately following years.

Apse and choir: as we have said at the beginning, the apsidal part was extended towards the end of the 16th century. The fresco by *Correggio* depicting *The Coronation of the Virgin amongst the Sts. John the Evangelist, Benedict, Mauro and John the Baptist* was therefore destroyed.

What we see in the new apse is a copy frescoed in 1586 by *Cesare Aretusi,* while the central part of the original fresco, with the figures of *Christ* and the *Virgin* is preserved in the *National Gallery*.

Behind the high altar the enormous altarpiece portrays *The Transfiguration*. *Gerolamo Bedoli Mazzola* painted it in 1556, inspired by the similar work by *Raphael* that is preserved in the *Pinacoteca Vaticana*. The gilded niche is a work by the brothers *Gianfranco* and *Pasquale Testa*.

Correggio had painted also the lateral walls with figures of *Sibyls* and *Prophets*. Now they are hidden by the large chancels realized by *Pietro Cuppini* in 1636, when the organ was moved here.

The choir is a fine work of art and is composed of 69 stalls, 41 upper ones and 28 lower ones.

Church of St. John the Evangelist
1: The dome by Correggio
2: The apse
3: The choir

The splendid inlays depicting urban and rural landscapes, fruits, mechanisms, books and musical instruments, were executed for the most part by *Marcantonio Zucchi* (45 stalls) between 1512 and 1531, when he died.

The *Testa Brothers* took his place and terminated the remaining 24 stalls in 1538.

In the centre of the choir there is a large lectern sculptured in 1749 by *Andrea Boschi* on a design by *Giuseppe Bianchi*.

Left transept: like in the right transept, a frieze with sacrificial scenes realized in 1514 by *Giovanni Antonio da Parma* runs along it horizontally. In the Chapel beside the high altar, under the arch, a fresco carried out by *Michelangelo Anselmi* in 1523 with evident influences by *Parmigianino* portrays *St. Agnes*, on the left, and *St. Catherine,* on the right.

The altarpiece depicting *the transit of St. Benedict* is a work by *Antonio Barnabei,* while the tempera decorations depicting *scenes from the life of St. Bernard* are a work of the late 1700 by *Domenico Crivelli* and *Domenico Muzzi*.

Between the chapel and the entrance to the sacristy there's the third painted terracotta by Begarelli portraying *The Madonna with Child and St. Giovannino.* Under the sacristy door the renowned lunette realized in 1520 by *Correggio* stands out depicting *the Young St. John writing.*

Chapel of St. Mauro and St. Benedict: it's placed at the bottom of the transept.

In the apsidal bowl-shaped vault Anselmi portrayed *St. Benedict on throne amongst the Sts. Flavia, Placid, Maurus and Scholastica.*

The altarpiece painted in 1674 by *Emilio Taruffi* depicts *St. Maurus healing the plagued.* Going out, on the right it's possible to admire the fourth terracotta by Begarelli depicting *St. John the Evangelist.*

Left nave

Sixth chapel: it's dedicated to the *Bergonzi* family. Under the arch we can see *The Doctors of the Church, Adam and Eve driven away from Heaven, The Theological Virtues.* At first, the fresco was attributed to *Parmigianino,* but later on it was definitely cred-

Church of St. John the Evangelist
Cloister of St, John

ited to *Michelangelo Anselmi* due to the evident influences by the Sienese school.

The tablet painting portraying *Christ bearing the Cross* is also by Anselmi.

Fifth chapel: the allegoric scene *Noli me tangere* is attributed to Anselmi. It's a monochrome fresco that can be seen in the fascia under the arch.

Fourth chapel: it's dedicated to *St. Nicholas*, and it's one of the most evocative of the whole Basilica.

The Baroque frescoes depicting the *Stories of St. Nicholas* are fine works of art painted in 1685 by *G. B. Merano*.

In the under-arch, a fresco by a young *Parmigianino* depicts *St. Nicholas Bishop* on the right, and *St. Hilary* on the left.

The altarpiece is another fine work of art depicting *The mystical marriage of St. Catherine. Gerolamo Mazzola Bedoli* painted it in 1536.

Third chapel: it's dedicated to *St. John.* Giuseppe Boni carried out the fresco on the walls and the vault in 1729, portraying *Scenes from the life of the Saint.*

The altarpiece is attributed to the Flemish John *Sons*, and depicts *The Madonna with child amongst St. Steven Pope and John the Evangelist.*

In the external fascia of the under-arch, a monochrome fresco by Anselmi describes *The flagellation of Jesus and St. Lawrence.*

Second chapel: it's known as that *of the Crucifix.* The vault and the walls are decorated with frescoes by *G. Boni* and *B. Aldovrandini* portraying *The Cross taken in triumph by the Angels.*

The under-arch bears one of the first frescoes in the Basilica by *Parmigianino* (1521). On the right it depicts *St, Vitalis holding a horse* that seems to come out of the wall, while on the left we can admire *Two deacons while reading.*

First chapel: it's dedicated to *St. Gertrude.* The vault and the walls frescoed by Aldovrandini portray *Scenes from the life of the Saint.* On the under-arch a fresco by *Parmigianino* depicts *St. Agatha and the executioner and the Sts. Apollonia and Lucy.*

In this 1522 fresco it's possible to detect a certain influence by *Correggio*, who was then frescoing the dome.

The sacristy: the Milanese *Cesare Cesariano* frescoed it in 1508.

On the walls we can see depictions of the virtues and biblical scenes alternated with grotesques, while the ceiling is frescoed with round frames portraying valuable marbles.

Local craftsmen carried out the wooden covering of the walls.

In an octagonal room annexed to the sacristy in 1618, a fine wardrobe storing relics has doors painted by Anselmi with the figures of the *Sts. Sebastian and John the Baptist* on the outside, and grotesques on a blue background on the inside.

*Church of St. John the Evangelist
Cloister of the Chapter*

THE MONASTERY

It was built in the 16th century at the same time with the extension of the apsidal part of the Church, within the cultural activity boosting program.

This was justified by the need for wider spaces for debates and to accommodate the guests.

It's composed of *three cloisters*, which may be accessed by exiting the Church on the right.

Cloister of St. John: chronologically it's the last one (1537-38). It has a beautiful portico with Ionic columns. On the walls there are remains of 16th century-frescoes.

Cloister of the Chapter: chronologically it's the first one (1500), and is connected to the previous one thanks to the continuation of the perimeter ring. From the portico it's possible to access the *Chapter-house* by crossing a beautiful portal with shrines and two-light windows, a work by *Antonio Ferrari D'Agrate.* Inside, we can admire a fine wooden choir by *Marcantonio Zucchi* and a beautiful canvas painted in 1744 by *L. Peroni* depicting *The Madonna of the Rosary.*

Cloister of St. Benedict: it's the widest of the three and was built between 1508 and 1512. This is where the monks live. Their cells are on the upper floors.

The *Refectory* and the *Library* are both beautiful. The former is decorated with *The last Supper* painted in 1536 by *Gerolamo Mazzola Bedoli,* while the latter has three naves separated by two rows of Ionic columns, and stores precious *Miniated codices* and over *twenty* thousand ancient books.

Pharmacy-spice shop.

The one we see currently was built in the first years of 1500, but a pharmacy was already existing in 1201, at first intended only for internal service and later on opened to the public. It's composed of four halls.

The hall of fire: it owes its name to the large 16th century fireplace. It accommodates the counter for the deliveries, the scales, and ceramic vases dating back to the 16th and 17th centuries in the shelves. On the vault, a medallion carried out in 1606 by *Innocenzo Marini* depicts the *Assumption of the Virgin.*

Hall of the mortars: it may be accessed by entering a door surmounted by a wooden eagle, the symbol of the monastery. Shelves with ceramic vases and marble or bronze mortars may be found also in this hall. The lunettes portray the Scholars of Medicine, while in the centre of the vault a fresco depicts the *Apparition of the St. Trinity to St. John.*

Hall of the Sirens: it owes its name to the caryatids sculptured on the shelves, which store precious medicine and pharmacy volumes spanning from the 16th to the 19th century. The 17th-century lunettes enclose the portraits of Parmesan physicians of those times, while above the counter we may admire a beautiful painting of Ferrarese origin portraying a *Madonna with Child and the Sts. Benedict and John the Evangelist.*

Hall of the laboratory: it was precisely the laboratory of the pharmacy, and some alembics, stills and scales that were used to prepare the medicines are stored in an underlying room.

Church of St. John the Evangelist
Spice shop - the hall of the Mortars

H) ORATORY OF THE CONCEPTION

It was built between 1521 and 1531 as a chapel connected to the nearby *Monastery of St. Francesco al Prato;* one of its rows still exists, broken off in 1800.

It's one of the first temples of the city with a central base, in Renaissance style.

The decoration of the octagonal dome, the tambour, the pendentives and the vaults of the rows are a work by *Michelangelo Anselmi* and *Francesco Maria Rondani,* contributors of *Correggio.*

The frescoes portray scenes inspired by the dogma of the *Immaculate Conception,* and are showed as canvases supported by youngsters and maidens.

Antonio Borra realized the stuccoes on the capitals and the windows during a restructuring, in 1718. The decorations by *Giovanni Pelliccioli* date back to the same period.

On the high altar there are copies of the niche and the altarpiece depicting again the *Immaculate Conception;* the originals painted between 1531 and 1536 by *Gerolamo Mazzola Bedoli* are stored in the National Gallery.

On the bottom wall a fragment of a fresco coming from the Church of St. Francesco depicts a *Madonna with Child and the Sts. Francesco and John the Baptist.*

In the lateral chapels two beautiful canvases portray *The Child appearing to St. Anthony da Padova,* by *Francesco Monti,* on the right, and *St, Francesco receiving the stigmata,* by *Alessandro Mazzola Bedoli,* on the right.

Oratory of the Conception
1: The bell tower of the Basilic of St. Francesco al Prato, now seat of the University
2: The outside

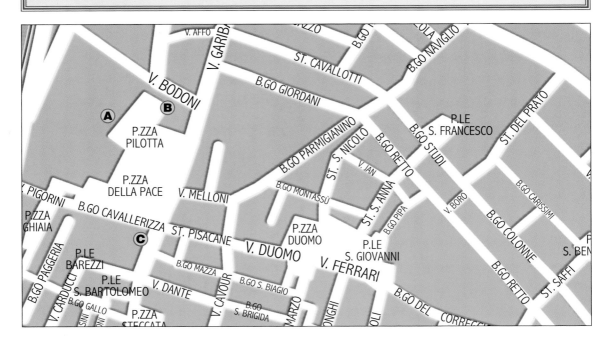

A) PALACE OF THE PILOTTA

Ranuccio I Farnese, Duke of Parma, had this enormous but uncompleted construction built in its current dimensions. He extended and completed what his grandfather *Ottavio* had previously built. The latter had the wing of the building facing *Piazza Ghiaia* _ known as the *Corridore* _ built starting from 1583. Nowadays it accommodates the *Bodoni Museum* and the *Palatina Library,* which we shall describe later.

In Ranuccio' concept, the building was to be intended not only as the seat of the services of the then nearby Court to accommodate the Barracks, the stables, the warehouses, the State Archive, the mint and the armoury, later on changed into a theatre, but also as a protected passage to reach the Ducal Park, across the river. The Farnese used to cross it thanks to a bridge closed to the public.

The works of the first core, the project of which had been entrusted to the architect *Francesco Paciotto* from Urbino, were interrupted in 1586, when the Duke Ottavio died.

Works were resumed in 1602 with Ranuccio, who directly participated also in the design. The Court engineer *Simone Moschino* was responsible for the design.

The wing that already been built was held as the starting point for the new building, which took on the majestic designing reference.

The first courtyard to be built was the one in the lee of the pre-existing building. It was originally called of *St. Peter Martyr*, as it included the Dominican Monastery that was therefore incorporated in the new building. It is now called *Courtyard of the Pilotta*, because the former Monastery was destroyed in 1813 by Napoleon's troops.

The other two courtyards were realized later on: the larger one, where horses were watered, was named *of the guazzatoio*, while the other one was called *of the roc-*

54

chetta because the pre-existing *Fortress of the Visconti* was incorporated in it. Parts of it can still be seen on the side facing the river.

In 1611 works were interrupted and never resumed, although there was more than one project, not only by Moschino but also by another two architects, *the* Bolognese *Pier Francesco Battistelli* and the Roman *Gerolamo Raimondi.*

With Ranuccio's death in 1622 all the projects were abandoned and thus the building remained uncompleted.

The project of the octagonal dome is almost certainly owed to Moschino. It gives light to the *Imperial Stairway,* consisting of three flights of stairs and inspired by the one of the *Escorial* in Madrid, which had fascinated Ranuccio.

The *Bourbons,* whom replaced the *Farnese,* did not carry out structural interventions, but carried out modifications only in the inside to accommodate the museums and libraries, which are still in it. But the Bourbons had the Ducal dwellings placed against the new building demolished, to build a new one on a project by the Court architect *Petitot.* But this construction was never built, and the rent opened as a consequence towards Via Garibaldi was partially arranged by *Marie Louise.* She had the facade and the portal in front of the main stairway redone by *Nicola Bettoli.*

1: The enormous mass of the building seen from Piazza della Pace
2: The imposing porticoes.

1) National Archaeology Museum

The creation of the first core of this museum occurred in 1768 thanks to the patronage of *Philip of Bourbon* and his prime minister *Du Tillot.* The passion of both for whatever could make Parma more and more important started off with the finding of the *Tabula Alimentaria* - one of the largest bronze inscriptions of the ancient times - during excavation works, together with statues and other finds that were part of the Roman city

of *Veleia. Antonio Costa* first, then *Paolo Maria Paciaudi* catalogued and reordered all the gathered material. The latter is responsible for other findings in *Luceria* (Reggio Emilia). *Pietro Del Lama* continued their work. He may be considered the real founder of the museum, notwithstanding the difficulties he had to face because of the Napoleonic domination when he became the director of the museum in 1799. The treaty of Vienna gave sovereignty back to the Duchy, therefore De Lama could reorder the museum, acquiring also the *Inscriptions of Piacenza that* were found in the *Church of St. Augustine*, and the treasure found in 1821 during the excavation works for the construction of the *Royal Theatre. Michele Lopez* replaced De Lama when the latter died in 1825. The former directed the museum until 1867, enriching the collection with Greek and Egyptian findings thanks to

Palace of the Pilotta
1: The Imperial Stairway and the entrance to the
   Farnese Theatre
2: The octagonal dome
Archaeology museum
3: Hall 6 - The Tabula Alimentaria from Veleia

donations. In 1842 the museum was enriched with some findings from a *Roman Theatre* discovered in via Farini, in Parma, during excavations works to arrange the hydric network. In 1866 he obtained from the *Academy* the 12 statues found in *Veleia.*

When De Lama died in 1867 *Luigi Pigorini* was appointed as director. He managed the museum until 1875, creating the core of the *prehistoric collections.*

From 1875 until 1933, almost sixty years, the direction of the museum was entrusted to *Giovanni Mariotti,* who further enriched the collections, although displaying them in a disorderly manner without considering the periods and the areas of origin. The current arrangement was actuated starting from 1934, under the direction of *G. Monaco* first, then of *P. Mansuelli.* The visit to the museum begins on the *first floor.*

Hall 1: it accommodates classical sculptures coming for the most part from the *Gonzaga Collection* of Guastalla; among them an enormous head of *Zeus* stands out.

Hall 2: it displays the *Egyptian Collection* gathered by Lopez, which consists of alabaster vases, sarcophagi, funereal papyruses and relieves, as well as a mummy.

Hall 3: it contains findings of *Greek origin* coming from the Farnese and Gonzaga collections, as well as some *Attic vases* found in *Vulci.*

Hall 4: it is known as that *of the medals* because it accommodates a collection of over 20,000 golden, silver and bronze pieces spanning from the Greek age to modern times.

The collection of coins is also notable.

Hall 5: the 12 statues found in Veleia are gathered here.

Hall 6: it displays the *bronze findings* of *Veleia.* The most important one is the *Tabula Alimentaria, which* is extremely important from a historic standpoint because it lists the farms that had received loans from the *Emperors Nerva* and *Trajan,* the interests of which benefited the poor. Moreover, it stores the table of the *Lex de Gallia Cisalpina* concerning the competencies of the Magistrates in the Republican period. In the showcases there are other bronze findings, among which the *Inebriated Hercules* stands out. His club was found only during recent excavations.

Hall 7: it accommodates *Etruscan findings* dating back to the Hellenistic period. Along the stairway that leads to the ground floor there's a room that stores *epigraphs* from various periods.

Ground floor

Hall 1: it contains manufactures from the *Palaeolithic, Neolithic and Aeneolithic periods.*

Hall 2: it contains findings from the surrounding *marshlands.* These objects were part of the everyday life of the *dwellers of the palafitte.*

Hall 3: it's dedicated to *Luigi Pigorini* and accommodates objects from the *bronze age* found by Pigorini himself during the excavations in Parma and its surroundings. The halls at the right hand side of the atrium store Roman gravestones, bronzes, funereal monuments and milestones coming from excavations carried out both in the city and its surroundings.

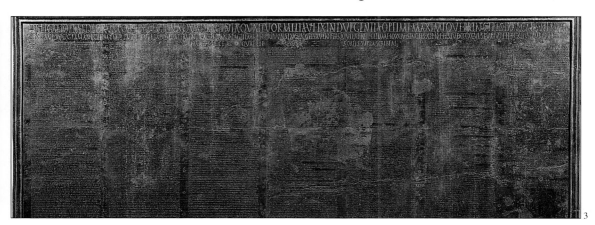

2) Farnese Theatre

It was built in a rush between 1617 and 1619 in the former armoury of the Pilotta, located on the first floor. *Ranuccio I Farnese* had it built to show *Cosimo I Medici* - whose visit had been announced - the luxury of his court. The intention was to have closer political relations with the powerful Florentine family.

With this purpose he also tried to favour the marriage between the son *Odoardo* and Cosimo's daughter, *Margherita.*

In order to speed up the times the architect *Giovan Battista Aleotti* from Argenta, who had been entrusted with the task to conceive and realize a very scenic theatre, used wood instead of bricks for the structures, scagliola instead of marble for the statues and painted cardboard in place of decorative stuccoes.

The work was then continued and finished by *Enzo Bentivoglio* and *Giovan Battista Magnani.* Notwithstanding the rushed construction this theatre is a real masterpiece, because it couples the majesty of the more sober Renaissance style with the fantasy of the rising Baroque, used in many details.

Moreover, movable sets were used instead of fixed ones, anticipating the concept of modern theatres.

Under Ranuccio's continuous incitement the theatre became a lot more capacious and luxurious with respect to what court theatres had been until then.

It may be entered by crossing a wooden portal painted as fake marble and surmounted by a large frieze where the *Ducal Crown* is inserted.

The *cavea* is surrounded by a large wooden balustrade and is interrupted in the centre by the majestic entrance to the underlying vestibule and by two stairways leading to the 14 large steps of the circle. A double tier of 17 loggias rest on the last step, the upper ones separated by Doric columns and the lower ones by Ionic ones.

Each of the 34 loggias has small rounded arches supported by two elegant small columns; on the upper corners there are medallions with Greek and Roman effigies. An elegant balustrade lies above the two tiers of loggias. The *stage* is enclosed in a Corinthian-style proscenium, and is as large as the whole of the stalls, which for the first time are positioned in the shape of a horseshoe rather than that of a semicircle. The *stalls,* with no benches or seats, actually become a part of the stage, bringing the scenes and the actors a lot nearer to the public that could therefore be more involved in the show.

A clever machine system was installed under the stage allowing for the first *movable sets* in the history of theatre.

Above the *proscenium*, a large Ducal coat of arms is surmounted by Latin writings dedicated to the Muses protecting the Arts. Between the tiers of seats and the stage

two triumphal arches bear the equestrian statues of the *Duke Ottavio,* on the right, and of the *Duke Alessandro*, on the left.

The ceiling was unfortunately destroyed. It was frescoed with the image of *Jupiter* surrounded by the Gods with an azure sky as background. Sad to say, even the two enormous pendant chandeliers with 300 candles each were destroyed.

The theatre was inaugurated only 10 years later, on December the 21st 1628, on the occasion of the long-awaited wedding between *Odoardo Farnese* and *Margherita de' Medici*, with the play *Torneo*.

Although the luxury of the inauguration could lead one to think of an intense artistic activity, the theatre was scarcely used both by the Farnese and the Bourbons, and the last show took place in 1732.

At first *Marie Louise* and then *Giovanni di Savoia* had restorations performed, especially on the roof, but the state of abandonment inexplicably continued.

During the last conflict a bombing grievously damaged the theatre.

Reconstruction began immediately after the war, also using the original materials whenever it was possible to recover them.

Farnese Theatre - the cavea

3) National Gallery

In 1734 *Don Charles of Bourbon*, who had become *King of the two Sicilies*, had all the paintings, furnishings and decorations of the various Ducal courts transported to Naples, the seat of the new court. The new Duke, *Don Philip of Bourbon*, tried to recreate the local artistic patrimony, helped in this by the prime minister *Du Tillot*. He therefore established the *Academy of Fine Arts*, still in the halls of the Pilotta, and had the new purchases, carried out mainly in Tuscany, transported there together with the *Madonna of St. Jerome* by *Correggio*. The latter had been taken from the city Church of St. Anthony. The son, *Don Ferdinand*, continued his work and brought in new prestigious collections, among which the extremely important one of the *Tuscan Primitives*, purchased from the *Taccoli-Canacci* family. *Marie Louise* had many of the works of art plundered by Napoleon returned to Parma, and with *Paolo Toschi*'s precious co-operation she enriched the collection by purchasing the private collections of the *Sanvitale, Callani, Bajardi Rossi* and *Dalla Rosa Prati* families. Moreover, she had the halls of the Pilotta restored by the court architect *Nicola Bettoli*, and she arranged there all the new artistic patrimony according to well-defined concepts. In 1882 the collection was no longer a responsibility of the Academy of Fine Arts, and in 1945 it became the *National Gallery*. A new and final arrangement of the museum was started in the following years, incorporating in it the whole wing of the building facing the *courtyard of the guazzatoio*. In practical terms there are two sections in the gallery: the first one is dedicated to *Parmesan painting*, with particular reference to the two great representatives of the 16th century, *Correggio* and *Parmigianino,* while the second one accommodates works by some of the most important Italian and foreign artists.

The oldest piece of the Parmesan section is the fragment of a 13th-century fresco from

National Gallery
1: Correggio: The Coronation of the Virgin
2: Correggio: The Madonna of the Bowl

1

the Cathedral. Among the Parmesan artist working until the 16th century, the following artists are worth mentioning *Jacopo Loschi, Cristoforo Caselli, Alessandro Araldi, Filippo Mazzola* (Parmigianino's father), *Gerolamo Mazzola Bedoli, Michelangelo Anselmi.* From the section dedicated to *Correggio* we should remember the fresco depicting the *Coronation of the Virgin;* the fresco portraying the *Madonna of the Stairway;* the *Mourning of the dead Christ* canvas; the *Deposition* canvas; the *Martyrdom of four Saints* canvas; the *Madonna of the Bowl* canvas; the *Madonna of St. Jerome*

National Gallery
1: Correggio: The Madonna of St. Jerome
2: Parmigianino: - the Turkish slave

2

canvas. Only two canvases by *Parmigianino* are left: *The Turkish slave* and a *Self-portrait.* On the back of the latter there's a pen drawing depicting *St. Catherine and the Madonna with Child.* Crossing the splendid *Farnese Theatre* one reaches the other section, which accommodates a display in neat chronological order and divided by schools. We would like to mention the following: The *Majestatis Domini,* a slab sculptured by Benedetto Antelami, *The doors of St. Berthold,* dating back to the 10th century, and some paintings by artists of the 14th- and 15th-century Tuscan school, such as

Agnolo Gaddi, Spinello Aretino, Beato Angelico, Bicci di Lorenzo, Giovanni di Paolo, Leonardo da Vinci.

From the Emilian school of the '600-'700 we would like to recall the works by *Annibale Carracci, Jacopo Carracci, Bartolomeo Schedoni, Giovanni Lanfranco, Guercino, Giuseppe Maria Crespi*.

The Genoese, Spanish and Flemish schools are represented in a special section with works by *G.A. De Ferrari, Murillo, A. Van Dick*.

From the Venetian school of the '700 we would like to recall the works by *Sebastiano Ricci, Tiepolo, Canaletto, Tintoretto*.

From the section dedicated to *Marie Louise* we will mention *Antonio Canova, G. Borghesi, S. Appiani, B. Martini, G. A. Pock*. The last section displays the works by artists of the late '800 and the early '900.

National Gallery
1: *Antonio Canova*
   Marie Louise depicted as Concord
2: *Jean Baptiste De Save - Alessandra Farnese*
3: *Giuseppe Boldrighi*
   Don Philip of Bourbon with the family

3

4) Palatina Library

It was established in 1761 as *Royal Parmesan Library*, within the program providing for the reconstitution of the city's artistic patrimony ordered by *Don Philip of Bourbon* and his prime minister *Du Tillot*.

Its constitution was entrusted to *Paolo Maria Paciaudi*, who was already taking care of the arrangement of the Archaeology Museum.

He had thousands of volumes sent in from all over Italy and Europe, cataloguing them for the first time in bibliographic history with *movable cards* and dividing them into six main classes: *Theology, Nomology, Philosophy, History, Philology, Liberal and Mechanic Arts.*

It was inaugurated in 1769, with *Joseph II of Austria* attending the ceremony.

Thanks to the passionate work of the director *Angelo Pezzana*, even *Marie Louise* gave a strong drive to the library. In 1865, with

Palatina Gallery: the first hall

Italy already united by the Savoia, it was named *Palatina* because in the meantime it had acquired the collection of the manuscripts and the prints of the *Dukes of Bourbon Parma,* of relevant importance.

The first majestic hall displays walnut shelves designed by *Petitot* and a coffer-painted ceiling.

They were partially redone because the hall was damaged during an air bombing in the last war.

The second hall, known as that *of the Coronation*, stores the *sinopite* of the fresco by *Correggio* that decorated the apse of the Basilica of St. John the Evangelist, before it was demolished.

The *Dante hall*, which owes its name to the frescoes portraying episodes from the *Divine Comedy* that decorate the walls and the ceiling, accommodates the precious *Ortalli collection*, composed of over 40,000 prints and engravings by great artists.

One then reaches large *Reading hall of Marie Louise, built* in 1834 on a design by *Nicola Bettoli.* It has wide shelves, a coffered ceiling and stucco medallions, and contains over 16,000 volumes.

The marble bust portraying Marie Louise is a fine work of art by *Antonio Canova.*

The current *De'Rossi Hall,* where the most precious material of the library is stored, was rebuilt in 1894, after the one facing the current *Piazza della Pace* had been demolished to allow for an easier traffic flow.

5) Bodoni Museum

It was established in 1963 and placed on the last floor of the Palatina Gallery.

It's dedicated to *Giambattista Bodoni*, an eminent engraver, typographer and editor from Saluzzo who was summoned to Parma in 1768 by *Don Ferdinand of Bourbon* to found and direct the *Royal Printing works.*

Bodoni is also famous for having designed a new character that is still called the *Bodoni type*. He created a first-class graphic workshop that was then internationally renown.

The hall gathers the tools he used, the volumes he printed and manuscripts and books by Italian and foreign typographers in touch with him, that may help to understand the evolution of the graphic art.

B) ALTAR DEDICATED TO GIUSEPPE VERDI

This monument was part of a mausoleum placed in the square facing the railway station, inaugurated in 1920.

During the last war it was damaged only slightly, but this was enough to give building speculation the chance to demolish it.

Only the altar could be transported to its current location, and it is immediately evident at sight that this location is certainly not the ideal one.

The author of the bronze part is *Hector Ximenes,* and portrays the Maestro standing out with a thoughtful expression amongst elegant allegoric characters representing the Arts.

In the back, low relieves depict historic events of the Risorgimento connected with the Maestro's work: among them we should note the one with the cartel bearing the famous writing *Viva Verdi.*

1: Bodoni Museum: the first press of Bodoni
2: The altar dedicated to Giuseppe Verdi

C) ROYAL THEATRE

Marie Louise had it built between 1821 and 1829. She entrusted its design to the ducal architect *Nicola Bettoli*.

She wanted to endow Parma with a modern structure like the one of other cities such as the *Scala* of Milan, the *Fenice* of Venice and the *S. Carlo* of Naples.

The old Ducal Theatre, located in the Palace of the *Riserva*, no longer suited the requirements of modern theatres that required movable sets on the stage and overlapping boxes in the walls of the cavea, in order to accommodate a larger number of people and give higher emphasis to the *Royal Box*.

The new Ducal Theatre was inaugurated on May the 16th 1829 with the opera *Zaira*, by *Vincenzo Bellini*. It was named *Royal Theatre* only in 1849.

Those were the years when *Giuseppe Verdi* was beginning to have success. He was born in the nearby Busseto in 1813, thus the *Royal Theatre* became one of the temples of opera music, and its public one of the most refined.

The neo-classic facade has a portico supported by ten Ionic columns and is surmounted by two fascias.

1: The outside
2: The stage with the painted curtain by Borghesi, seen from the royal box.

1

Low relief sculptures by *Tommaso Bandini* appear in the upper one and in the triangular tympanum.

The vestibule has eight Ionic columns supporting a fine ceiling with beams decorated with stuccoes.

The horse shoe-shaped stalls have four tiers of boxes and the gallery.

In the centre there's the luxurious Royal box.

The boxes at the sides of the proscenium are enclosed in friezes containing medallions, in which the portraits of musicians and poets of those times are inserted.

The beautiful proscenium with a coffered architrave has a luxurious curtain portraying *The triumph of Minerva,* a work by *Giovan Battista Borghesi.*

Girolamo Magnani carried out the white-and-gilded stucco decoration in 1853.

Royal Theatre
The stalls and the boxes seen from the stage.

ITINERARY No. 4
A) Ducal Park • B) Ducal Palace, *Ducal Park* • C) Church of the Holy Cross, *Piazzale S. Croce* • D) Church of St. *Francesco di Paola, Via M. D'Azeglio* • E) Arturo Toscanini Home Museum, *Via R. Tanzi* • F) Oratory of Our Lady of Graces, *Via Farnese* • G) Old Hospital, *Via M. D'Azeglio* • H) Oratory of St. Hilary, *Via M. D'Azeglio* • I) Church of Out Lady of the Assumption, *Via M. D'Azeglio* • L) Church of St. Mary of the Quarter, *Piazza Picelli*

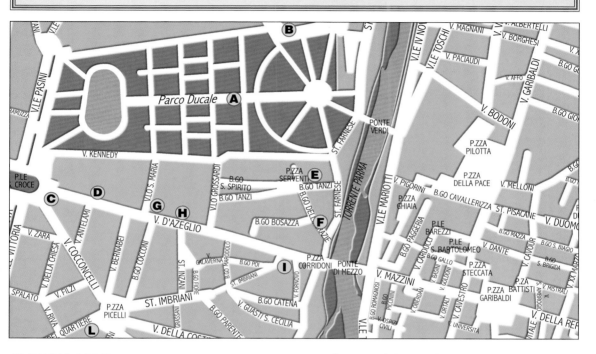

A) DUCAL PARK

By crossing the *G. Verdi Bridge* behind the Pilotta one reaches this beautiful garden wanted by *Ottavio Farnese* because he had decided to settle in Parma, and therefore he wanted to endow it with everything a Ducal Court required.

In order to build a suitable Summer residence he therefore purchased a large area across the *Parma Stream*, also with the purpose of curing the degraded and abandoned condition it was in at the time. He entrusted the design for the realization of the park and the summer residence to the architect *Jacopo Barozzi*, from Modena, known as *Vignola*. Initially the garden was arranged on the model of the large Italian villas, but was modified later on.

In 1690, on the occasion of the wedding between *Odoardo Farnese* and *Dorotea of Neuburg,* a lake with a diameter of about 500 meters was excavated in the terminal part, with a small isle in the centre.

After a period of abandonment, in the mid-18th century *Philip of Bourbon* and his prime minister *Du Tillot* entrusted the court architect *Petitot* with the task of rearranging the park. The French specialist *Costant d'Ivry* worked with him.

The park then took on a more French appearance. Those were the years when both the *Templet of Arcadia* - which was the meeting place for the Academics of the Arcadia - and the ten marble statues by *G. B Boudard* were realized and placed in the small woods and in front of the Ducal Palace.

During her reign *Marie Louise* opened the park to the public. In 1866, under the *Savoia* rule, it became the *Municipal Park*.

In 1905 the entrance to the Verdi Bridge was opened, and the bastions were demolished.

In 1920 the fountain with three pools called *of the Parma* - but commonly called *of the Trianon* because it imitates a similar fountain in *Versailles* - was placed on the isle at the centre of the lake.

The pools and the marble group in the centre, deprived of many statues, came from the Palace of Colorno.

On that occasion hedges were modified and benches were installed according to a design by the scenographer *Giuseppe Carmignani.*

Ducal Park
1: A spot in the park
2: The Templet of Arcadia
3: The Trianon fountain

B) DUCAL PALACE

It may be entered by walking along a wide path. In front of the palace we find four of the ten statues by Boudard, which portray the geniuses *Vertumno* and *Pomona* on the right, and *Pale* and *Trittolemo* on the left. The building is a classic example of Vignola's work with its small tower on the central body. Originally there were two marble stairways leading directly to the *piano nobile* were we now find the portal and the balcony.

On the ground floor, instead of the current portal, a decorated grotto faced a bridge crossing a small lake in front.

In the first years of 1600 the building, which had until then merely consisted of the central body by Vignola, was extended by adding the other two bodies and the lateral courtyards, on a design by *Simone Moschino* and *Gerolamo Rainaldi.*

Further modifications were added in 1767 by the architect *Petitot*, who built the internal stairway and added the mezzanine to the two lateral avant-corps, rising them by a floor thus lending to the whole a more clas-

sical appearance. The building was scarcely used, both by the Bourbons and by Marie Louise, because they preferred the nearer and more luxurious palaces of Colorno and Sala for their summer holidays.

Now the palace accommodates the local Carabinieri Station.

Inside

On the ground floor three halls accommodate remains of frescoes by *C. Baglioni.* Going up the stairs one reaches the central hall of the *piano nobile,* known as that *of the birds* due to the presence on the ceiling of as much as 204 birds made of stucco, modelled by *Benigno Rossi* in 1767, during Petitot's restructuring. There is also a statue of Marie Louise.

From the hall it's possible to enter the rooms completing the *piano nobile.* Let's start from the first one in chronological

1: J.B. Boudard - The group of Sileno
2: J.B. Boudard - The genius Trittolemo
Page 74-75. Aerial view of the Ducal Palace

order, placed at the bottom on the left.

Orpheus' hall: the Bolognese *Girolamo Mirola* and his Parmesan pupil *Jacopo Zanguidi*, known as *Bertoja,* frescoed it between 1568 and 1570.

The hall is so called because the pictorial cycle was thought to represent the *Tale of Orpheus,* while in reality it portrays the meeting between *Ruggero and the magician Alcina,* descibed by *Ludovico Ariosto* in the 7th canto of the *Orlando Furioso.* Starting from the left wall, we see the arrival of Ruggero received by the magician with a portico as background. The following walls depict the *merry play* of the dames and knights, who are accompanied to their

rooms by pageboys, and other issues not included in the cycle.

On the vault. Ruggero and Alcina are busy reading surrounded by guests.

Hall of the kiss or of the *Aetas Felicior*: it was frescoed between 1570 and 1573, probably by Zanguidi alone because Mirola died in 1570.

The room is peculiar because of the presence of transparent columns, a novelty for those times. They were placed there to create a naturalistic illusion suiting the decorations on the walls and the vault, which portray love and chivalry scenes taken form the poem by *Boiardo* that narrates the love and war adventures of the *Paladin Orlando*.

In the centre of the vault, in a bay enclosed in a frame with the writing *Aetas Felicior*, *Venus* stretches forward towards the young *Cupid.*, Love scenes, horse rides and other episodes of the happy age surround the bay.

Hall of Erminia: unfortunately, only a few fragments remain of the fresco realized by in 1628 by the Bolognese *Alessandro Tiarini* inspired by the *Gerusalemme Liberata.* It's possible to see only the meeting between *Erminia* riding a horse and a dying *Tancredi.* Around the alcove we can admire a beautiful interlacing of stuccoes, from which a *Cupid* with a dove in his hand stands out. It's a work by *Carlo Bossi.*

Hall of Love: the frescoes on the vault were started in 1602 by the Bolognese *Agostino Carracci*, who died the following year and left the work uncompleted.

Of his work, only the central octagon remains portraying *Venal Love* by means of three cupids preparing the bow. On the right *Motherly love* is depicted with Aeneas and the mother Venus on a ship's prow, while on the left Mars and Venus by a sea rock represent *Celestial Love.* Above the window, *Peleus and Teti* covered with fish scales represent *Humanly love.* The stuccoes by *Luca Reti* were realized in 1608 and portray *Jupiter's loves. Carlo Cignani* frescoed the walls in 1680, with scenes concerning once again love. On a wall we may see the *Rape of Europa.* In the following ones, *Bacchus offers the treasure to Ariadne, The triumph of Venus and Cupid, The fight between Cupid and Pan.*

Hall of the legends: there are three walls frescoed between 1604 and 1619 by *Gian Battista Trotti*, known as *Malosso.* On the first one, *Jupiter meets Bacchus and Venus;* on the second one, *The sacrifice of Alcestis;* in the third one, *Circe re-gives human form to the comrades of Ulysses after having changed them into pigs;* on the fourth wall, at the sides of the window, two landscapes by the Flemish *John Sons.*

Ducal Palace: - Aetas Felicior hall:
1-2: Bertoja - details of the frescoes. In photograph 1 notice the kiss see through the play of the transparent columns.

C) CHURCH OF THE HOLY CROSS

This Romanesque Church was built in 1210 and consecrated in 1222, becoming the stop in Parma for the Pilgrims on the Via Francigena.

The architect *Jorio da Erba* had carried out the design. Between 1635 and 1666, following the collapse of the vault, restorations were performed that implied the raising of the naves, the construction of the dome and the presbytery and the adding of the *Chapel of St. Joseph*.

Between 1904 and 1909 restorations were performed to recreate the original Romanesque style of the outside.

The only original parts left are the central portal and the friezes surmounting it, on the outside, and the columns, the pilasters and the capitals in the inside.

The central portal of the facade is surmounted and sided by blind arches. Above the cornice there's a large central window, and in the tympanum a circular rosette. The inside is divided in three naves, separated by columns and pilasters with capitals, eight lower ones and four upper ones.

Giovanni Maria Conti and *Francesco Reti* painted the frescoes around the mid-17th century. The counter-facade portrays *The wedding of Canaan;* along the central nave we can see scenes of the *Sacred Family;* on the dome, *The Coronation of St. Mary amongst Angels;* on the pendentives, *St. Jerome, St. Elizabeth and St. John, a Prophet and a Sybil.* On the arc of triumph there's the *Annunciation.*

The 12 capitals bear vegetal trophies, figures and animals, partly fantastic, that were typical of the late Lombard Romanesque. The figures are rather rough, and not refined like the ones of the Cathedral, although almost contemporary.

Chapel of St. Joseph: it was frescoed by Conti as well. The vault shows *St. Joseph, the Virgin and the Holy Trinity.*

Starting form the right, on the walls we can see *The escape to Egypt, The slaughter of the Innocents, the Worship of the Magi, The birth of Jesus, Scenes form the life of St. Joseph.*

Presbytery: the chancels and the organ, realized in 1785 by *Odoardo Panini,* are made of carved wood and painted as marble. The high altar and a reliquary altar placed on the bottom wall are from the 18th century as well.

Sacristy: it has an octagonal shape, and its walls and the vault bear frescoes depicting *The Virgin in glory with the Child,* by *Francesco Rubini.*

D) CHURCH OF ST. FRANCESCO DA PAOLA

The facade is all that is left of this construction built in 1625 by the Minim Friars. The architect *Virginio Draghi* from Piacenza built it in Baroque style in 1689. Various occurrences led the building to be deconsecrated and be used at first as a mental home and then as children's hospital. It 1936 it was transferred to the University that made it the seat of the scientific faculties.

E) ARTURO TOSCANINI HOME MUSEUM

It's a modest building were the Maestro was born in 1867.

On the occasion of the centennial celebration of his birth, the heirs donated both the house and all the relics that now compose the museum to the Municipality. Among them we find collection of letters to Carducci, Respighi, and D'Annunzio, as well as the moulds of the Maestro's face and hands.

Church of the Holy Cross
1: The church seen form the square with the same name, on the right Via D'Azeglio with the towers of St. Francesco da Paola.
2: The sober inside
3: Home Museum Toscanini, the facade
4: The two towers, known as "of the Paolotti"

F) ORATORY OF ST. MARY OF GRACES

It was built on a design by the court architect *G.B. Magnani* within the restoration program of the Oltretorrente area, to accommodate a painting of the Virgin by an unknown author that was considered miraculous. In 1644 a restructuring was performed on a design by *Gerolamo Rainaldi,* during which the octagonal lantern above the presbytery was built, and the position of the entrance was inverted.

The building has a central plan, and the facade has a nice Baroque portal surmounted by straight and arched friezes.

The inside is subdivided in a central part and two lateral chapels, with dividing pilasters decorated with gilded shells. The decorations covering the whole of the inside are in Baroque style, with fake architectures and other squaring elements realized in 1715 by *Francesco Natali.* The dome was inspired by those of *Correggio* and portrays the *Assumption of the Virgin* amongst a crowd of Angels and putti. The prophets *David, Daniel, Isaiah and Samson* appear on the pendentives. *Sebastiano Galeotti* realized the dome and the pendentives in 1715.

Above the marble high altar we find the canvas of the *Blessed Virgin of Graces,* while on the walls there are fine chancels in carved and gilded wood with caryatids.

Behind the altar a beautiful coloured terracotta group by *Giuseppe Sbravati* depicts the *Dead Christ.*

In the right chapel, a beautiful painting by *Antonio Savazzini* depicts the *Madonna presenting the Child to St. Francesco,* while in the left one we can admire a fine canvas executed by *Sisto Badalocchio* in 1621 portraying *The Guardian Angel piercing the Devil.*

G) OLD HOSPITAL

It's also known as *hospital of mercy. Rodolfo Tanzi* founded it in 1201 as a shelter for the ill and the infirm, using a building he had received as present from a priest. In the following years it also became a refuge for orphans.

In 1471, following a decree by *Pope Sisto IV,* all the hospitals in Parma were reunited, and it was decided to build a new large hospital in place of the old one. Works began in 1476 under *Gian Antonio Erba* guidance,

who directed them until his death in 1507. *Gaspare Fatuli* continued them.

The new large building that can still be seen now has a Renaissance style and the shape of a cross between cloisters, like the Florentine one *Degli Innocenti* built by *Brunelleschi*. Decorations were entrusted to *Antonio Ferrari D'Agrate* and *Maestro Geminiano Pittore*, who realized them between 1491 and 1505.

The hospital was further extended eastwards during the 16th century, in order to be able to accommodate the increasing number of ill people and orphans.

In 1663 the small *Oratory of St. Hilary* was built near the entrance to the vegetable garden. During the 18th century the southern part was changed from Church to infirmary. *Ferdinand I of Bourbon* ordered the realization of the new facades and the stairway, which were realized in 1780 on a design by the court architect *Luis Auguste Feneuille*.

In 1782, as stated by a memorial stone on the stairway, the northern wing of the building was considerably extended, and the court sculptor *J. Baptiste Cousinet* realized the four statues that are now in the National Gallery.

In 1843 *Marie Louise* had the western part of the building modified to use it as boarding place for the Nuns of St. Vincent who worked in the hospital.

Since 1926, when the hospital was closed, the building was dedicated to public use. It now accommodates the State archive, the Municipal library and craftsmen workshops.

H) ORATORY OF ST. HILARY

As we have mentioned above, it was built in 1663 and dedicated to the city's patron saint as ordered by the hospital's administrator, *Don Francesco Roncaglia*.

The facade has three portals: the central one is bigger and surmounted by an entablature, while the two smaller lateral ones are surmounted by two lunettes portraying *St, Bovo*, on the left, and *St. Nicomede and St. Vincent*, on the right.

The inside is divided in three naves by six square pilasters with capitals. They are decorated with cherubs and animals, and sup-

port the beautiful cross-vaults. It was completely frescoed between 1664 and 1666 by *Giovanni Maria Conti* and *Francesco Reti* with skies on which the figures of Saints and Blessed citizens stand out.

The apse is square and decorated with stuccoes by *Domenico Reti*. A niche encloses the wooden statue of *St. Hilary with texture vestments*.

On the left of the altar we find the carved wood sarcophagus of *Rodolfo Tanzi*, the founder of the hospital, realized by *Antonio Ferrari D'Agrate*.

Domenico Reti carried out the two groups symbolizing *Religion*, on the right, and *Charity*, on the left.

1: The oratory of St, Mary of Graces
2: Old Hospital: the entrance and the stairway
3: Oratory of St. Hilary. The central nave

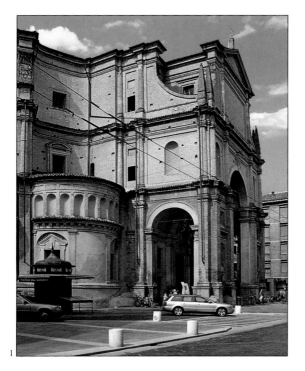

I) CHURCH OF OUR LADY OF THE ASSUMPTION

The construction works *began* in 1566, once again within the program by *Ottavio Farnese* for the valorization of the Oltretorrente area. The project was entrusted to the architect *Gian Battista Fornovo,* a contributor of Vignola, on whose example he drew up the project with an oval base and the entrance in the shorter axis.

A high portico characterizes the facade.

Above the central large arch the bare facade terminates with a triangular tympanum. On the sides of the portico we find the first two of the ten chapels that have apses falling outside the high walls of the central building's body, thus lending it a higher slenderness.

In the pronao, above the central portal, a large stucco depicting the *Eternal Father looking Our Lady of the Annunciation amongst Angels* is a work of 1680 by *Giovan Battista Barberini.*

The inside consists of a single nave that terminates in the large choir. It has very high Corinthian pilaster strips, between which the ten lateral chapels open and insert themselves in the vaulting ribs.

There are two fine marble holy water stoups, dating back to the 17th century.

On the right of the entrance, a large canvas depicts *The Consul Aspagio while ordering the body of St. Jarvis to be dragged in front of the brother St. Protaso.*

Beneath, a beautiful polychrome terracotta by *Giuseppe Sbravati* portrays *Ecce homo.*

On the first two pilasters there are frescoes by *Giulio Orlandini: St. Jerome and St. Luke,* on the right; *St. Augustine and St. Mark,* on the left.

First right chapel: the altarpiece by *Antonio Barnabei* depicts *The Virgin with Child and Saints.*

Second right chapel: the canvas portraying *St. Bonaventura kneeling down in front of the Virgin* is a work of 1720 by *Sebastiano Galeotti.*

Third right chapel: above the altar, a sculpture by several artists depicts *Our Lady of Sorrows at the feet of Jesus on the Cross.*

Fourth right chapel: above the altar, *The Madonna of Consolation* is a 17th-century canvas by an unknown artist.

Fifth right chapel: on the altar there is the statue of the *Sacred Heart.*

Presbytery: the floor and the altar are fine works of art with inlayed marbles, designed by *Antonio Brianti* and realized by *Giocondo Alberolli.*

The altarpiece above the altar depicting the *Virgin on Throne with Child and Saints* is a work of 1518 by *Francesco Paganelli*, who is also the author of the paintings that can be seen in the niche. The choir: it was frescoed by *Gerolamo Gelati*, and is composed of 51 stalls (31 upper ones and 20 lower ones), the backs of which are decorated with the coat of arms *Rolando Pallavicini*, who ordered it, and the *Franciscan Order*, which *also* appear on the two 18th-century chancels.

Between 1632 and 1634 the *Reti Brothers* realized the stucco above the arch of triumph, which portrays the *Annunciation*. They were also the authors of the decorations of the frieze with putti and the four statues of *Franciscan Saints*.

Two frescoes by *Girolamo Orlandini* depict *St. Ambrose and St. Matthew*, on the right, and *St. Gregory the Great and St. John*, on the left.

Fifth left chapel: above the altar and on the walls there are statues of Saints.

Fourth left chapel: the frescoes on the vault and the altarpiece, depicting *St. Peter of Alcantara* and episodes from his life, are works by *Ilario Spolverini*.

The two statues on the walls and the stucco decoration of the vault are by *Luca Redi*.

Third left chapel: the statues on the walls portraying *The Prophet Isaiah and St. John the Evangelist* are works of 1764 by *Gaetano Callani*, while the stucco statue of the *Immacu-late Conception* placed above the altar was realized by the *Ballanti-Graziani*.

Second left chapel: above the altar, the altarpiece of the *Blessed Giovanni Buralli* is a work of the late 1700 by *father Atanasio Favini*.

First left chapel: above the altar and on the walls there are papermache and stucco statues of various saints.

In the atrium by the door, the *Annunciation* by *Ignazio Affanni* is a copy of the original by *Correggio* that is now stored in the National Gallery.

Sacristy: the beautiful walnut pieces of furniture contain reliquaries and sacred vestments. The *Crucifix for the Via Crucis* is a fine 18th-century work of art by *Pietro da Betlemme*.

The medallions contain frescoed figures of Franciscan Saints.

Monastery: its construction began in 1566, at the same time with that of the Church, but works were interrupted several times. The *Refectory* was built in 1637 on a design by *G.B. Magnani,* and later on *Galeotti* frescoed it.

The *Cloister* was completed only in 1688.

The library stores more than 12,000 volumes, among which many incunabula and printed editions by *Bodoni*.

1: The pronao and the left side
2: The enormous stucco above the central portal
3: The majestic inside

L) CHURCH OF ST. MARY OF THE QUARTER

It owes its name to the fact that it was built in 1604 beside army quarters, on a design by *Gian Battista Aleotti*, and continued starting from 1610 by *Gian Battista Magnani,* who extended the choir and realized also the monastic complex.

The shape is that of a large hexagon with two overlapping bodies, divided by a cornice. On five corners there are enormous pilasters with capitals at the height of the cornice and buttresses on the upper part. On the sixth corner the slim and hexagon-based elegant bell tower stands out. The small chapel behind the high altar and the three avant-corps were built in the early 1700s.

The inside: *Pier Antonio Bernabei* frescoed the large dome between 1626 and 1629. In a fugue of concentric hexagons he depicted *Heaven,* with the Eternal Father, the Holy Ghost, Jesus and the Virgin on the summit, surrounded by figures of Saints, Prophets and Angels looking at them while ascending.

The domes of Correggio undoubtedly inspired Barnabei.

The tambour is decorated with monochrome figures of *Sibyls and Angels* frescoed in 1657 by *G. M. Conti.*

First right chapel: above the altar, the large statue of the *Madonna of Health* was sculptured in 1840 by *Tommaso Bandini.*

The frescoes depicting Saints and allegoric figures are by *Giovanni Gaibazzi.*

Second right chapel: *Francesco Scaramuzzi* painted the altarpiece in 1835 portraying the *Presentation to the temple.*

G. M Conti executed the frescoes in 1657 depicting *Jesus and Saints.*

Apsidal chapel*:* behind the high altar there's the fresco of the *Madonna of Abundance,* which was carried out in 1574 by *Mercurio Baiardi* on the wall of a house and later on taken in the Church because the Madonna was considered miraculous.

Second left chapel: *Giovanni Gaibazzi* carried out the altarpiece in 1842 portraying *Jesus healing the infirm.*

The frescoes portraying *The Virgin, some*

Saints and Biblical characters are works by G.M. Conti.

First left Chapel: *Tommaso Bandini* sculptured the statue of *St. Luis King of France* in 1841, under order by *Marie Louise.*

The frescoes, left uncompleted because of the death of Marie Louise - who was financing the work - are by *Giovanni Gaibazzi,* and portray chivalry characters.

1: The facade
2: A chapel

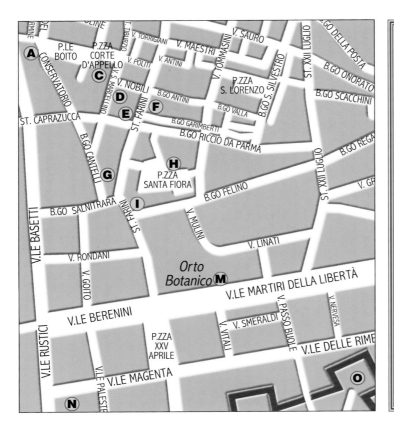

ITINERARY No. 5
A) Church of the Carmine, *Via del Conservatorio* • B) Arrigo Boito Conservatory, *Via del Conservatorio* • C) Palace of the Court, *Piazza Corte d'Appello* • D) Church of St. Marcellino, *Via Collegio dei Nobili* • E) Soragna Tarasconi Palace, *Via Farini* • F) Church of St. Thomas, *Via Farini* • G) Carmi Palace, *Via Farini* • H) Pallavicino Palace, *Piazzale S. Fiora* • I) Church of St. Uldarico, *Via Farini* • L) Church of St, Mary of the Angels, *Via Farini* • M) Botanical Garden, *Via Farini* • N) Chinese Museum, *Viale S. Martino* • O) *Cittadella, Via Passo Buole*

A) CHURCH OF THE CARMINE

It's in Gothic style, and the first foundation dates back to 1293.

The 14 chapels, new arches and the bell tower were built in the following centuries. In 1810 it was closed to worship, and unfortunately some fires destroyed the floor and some load-bearing structures, thus in 1813 it was decided to restore it, moving back the facade. It's now the seat of the State archive.

B) ARRIGO BOITO CONSERVATORY

It's located in the *Monastery of the Carmine*, and it's derived from the *Royal School of Music*, which was established in 1819 by *Marie Louise*. On *Niccolo Paganini*'s advice, in 1840 she ordered that the pupils of the singing school that was then the only operative one should have had to learn to play an instrument as well.

In 1888, also thanks to *Giuseppe Verdi'* intervention, its status was raised to that of a *Conservatory*, and since then it has been an out and out school of musical studies.

It's equipped with a very rich library composed of a collection of text books, manuscripts and original scores of works and songs by various authors, among which *Paganini, Boito, Leoncavallo* and *Toscanini*. It also accommodates *Ildebrando Pizzetti's* study.

C) PALACE OF THE COURT

It was built in 1855 on a design by *the* ducal architect *Nicola Bettoli.*
The facade is in fired brickwork and has variously styled windows.
Inside, two large stairways lead to the upper floors, where the wholly frescoed hall of hearings may be viewed.

D) CHURCH OF ST. MARCELLINO

It was built in 1533 on a design by *Giorgio da Erba.*
The straightforward facade shows Doric pilaster strips supporting the entablature and the pediment.
The inside has a single nave, and does not contain relevant works of art.

E) SORAGNA TARASCONI PALACE

The first foundation dates back to the last years of the 14th century, but the structure we see nowadays is the result of a design of 1580 by *Gian Francesco Testa*, who left many details of the facade uncompleted. Inside, the wide courtyard is enclosed in a portico surmounted by a Renaissance balcony, which may be accessed by going up an elegant helicoidal stairway. In the halls on the ground floor the vaults bear 17th-century frescoes, while the ones of the *piano nobile* have coffered ceilings.

1: The Palace of the Court
2: The Church of St. Marcellino
3: Soragna Tarasconi Palace
4: The Church of St. Thomas

F) CHURCH OF ST. THOMAS

The first foundation dates back to the beginning of the 11th century, and one side of the original building still exists. It was modified in 1786 on a design by *Carlo Bettoli*. The inside has a single nave with four Chapels per side, containing works by various artists. In the apse, a large canvas by *Alessandro Mazzola* portrays the *Nativity*.

1

3

2

4

G) CARMI PALACE

It was built between 1825 and 1830 on a design by the ducal architect *Paolo Gazzola,* on top of a pre-existent 16th-century building that can still be seen in the back part. The Neo-classic facade follows the curvilinear progress of Via Farini. It cannot be visited because it's private property. Nevertheless, it's possible to see the wide atrium, preceded by three arches, and the stairway with dome decorated with square sections and rosettes.

H) PALLAVICINO PALACE

Alfonso Pallavicino built it on a pre-existent 16th-century building starting from 1646. He had purchased it from the *Sforza di Santa Fiora* family. The facade has four floors, all with differently styled windows.

The entrance is preceded by two columns that support the balcony of the *piano nobile.* The large stairway starts from the beautiful Baroque-style courtyard. The former is decorated with statues in niches and surmounted by a fine and luminous dome frescoed by *G. Galeotti.*

The halls of the *piano nobile* are beautiful. They are all decorated with stuccoes, and have marble fireplaces surmounted by mirrors divided in bays.

1: Carmi Palace
2: Pallavicino Palace - The facade

I) CHURCH OF ST. ULDARICO

It was erected at the end of the 10th century on the ruins of the *Roman Theatre*, and the base of the bell tower belongs to this original building.

The reconstruction was performed around 1440 and decided by the Benedictine Nuns from Cassino that lived in the Convent. The secluded Cloister was constructed just then. It consists of a double order of arches divided by a fired brickwork cornice; there are pointed arches on the two shorter sides, and rounded arches on the two longer ones. The capitals alternatively present allegoric motifs and vegetal decorations. The Church was built in 1762, and a further redoing in 1902 implied the creation of the apse.

Inside, the counter-facade is frescoed with *St. Rocco among the infected with the plague*, painted in 1829 by *Giovanni Tebaldi*. In the three Chapels there are works by different artists.

Gaetano Ghidetti realized the chancel, the altar and the niche in the presbytery. The niche encloses a beautiful canvas depicting the *Sacred Family and the Saints Ulderico and Rocco,* which was carried out in 1742 by *Girolamo Donnini.*

On the sides of the apse two large canvases painted in 1718 by *Clemente Ruta* portray *Esther in front of Ahasuerus* and *Judith with the head of Holofernes.*

The choir and the lectern made of carved and inlayed wood are a work by *Gian Giacomo Baruffi.* He realized them starting from 1505 on order by the Abbess *Cabrina Carissimi.*

The sacristy also accommodates frescoes and paintings by various artists of those times.

Church of St. Uldarico
1: The facade
2: The inside

3: The porticoes in Via Farini

L) CHURCH OF ST. MARY OF THE ANGELS

It was built between 1565 and 1569 on a design by the architect *Gian Francesco Testa* to accommodate a strongly worshipped painting depicting a *Madonna with Jesus Child.*

The facade has a vestibule with a dome above the central portal.

The inside is subdivided into three naves separated by four red marble columns with white marble capitals, and is arranged transversally with respect to the entrance.

G. M. Conti frescoed the vaults of the three naves in 1620 with *scenes from the life of the Virgin and Jesus,* enclosing them in oval and octagonal frames, surrounded by Angels, Prophets and Sibyls.

In the same year P.A. *Bernabei* painted the two canvas medallions inserted in the central vault portraying again scenes from the life of May and Jesus.

G. B. Tinti frescoed the dome starting from 1588. At the summit we can see the *Dove of the Holy Ghost* surrounded by an extremely luminous halo, around which the figures of the *Eternal Father* and *Our Lady of the Assumption* stand out amongst a jubilation

of musician Angels. The whole of the work recalls the dome of the Cathedral by *Correggio,* but with livelier and more contrasting colours.

Moses, Ezekiel, Gideon and *Jesse appear* on the pendentives. On the apse above the high altar we find the *Pietà,* painted in 1685 by *Sebastiano Ricci.*

M) BOTANICAL GARDENS
It displays many types of plants from all over the world.

The *Parmesan* herbarium is extremely interesting for its completeness.

An important collection of scientific books may be consulted in the library, which is located in the elegant building in the centre of the garden.

N) CHINESE AND ETHNOGRAPHIC MUSEUM
It's accommodated in the *Palace of Foreign Missions* and stores the two collections mentioned in the title, which were gathered by missionaries. *Mons. Guido Maria Conforti,* the Bishop of Parma, had them catalogued. In this way he wanted to let the citizens and the pupil missionaries know the civilizations of the faraway countries where missions were operating. The *Chinese Collection* is particularly interesting. It includes bronzes, vases, ceramics and ivories spanning from the 3rd century BC to now.

Church of St. Mary of the Angels
1: The facade
2: The inside
3: The dome portraying Heaven, frescoed by G.B. Tinti

4: The Botanical Garden

Chinese Ethnographic Museum
5: Vase of the Ming Dynasty (16th cen. BC)
6: Bronze of the Ming Dynasty (16th cen. BC)

O) CITTADELLA

It was an out and out fortress with a large ditch surrounding the powerful bastions. It's shaped as a pentagon, and is certainly inspired by the one in *Antwerp*, because *Alessandro Farnese*, who had it built by the architects *Genesio Bresciani* and *Smeraldo Smeraldi*, was then the governor of the Flanders on behalf of *Philip II of Spain*.

It seems almost certain that the Duke personally took part in the design. Alessandro wanted to confirm the power of the Farnese family and his military skills, but works began in 1591 also to create some jobs for the population, who was then suffering from a terrible famine.

Terminated by Alessandro's son *Ranuccio*, the enormous structure was used as a prison at first and then as army barracks, rather than for actual defensive purposes. It is now used as a public park. Only the pentagonal walls and the entrance portal are left of the ancient structure. *G.B. Barra* built the portal on a design by *S. Moschino*.

1

1: Leisure activities in the park
2: The portal of St. Moschino

2

ITINERARY No. 6

A) Casinò Petitot, *Viale Martiri della Libertà* • B) Church of St. Quentin, *Via XXII Luglio* • C) Church of St. Christine, *Via Repubblica* • D) Dazzi Palace, formerly Corradi Servi, *Via Repubblica* • E) Rangoni Farnese Palace, *Via Repubblica* • F) Church of St. Antonio Abate, *Via Repubblica* • G) Marchi Palace (Institute of Verdi Studies), *Via Repubblica* • H) Church of the Holy Sepulchre, *Via Repubblica*

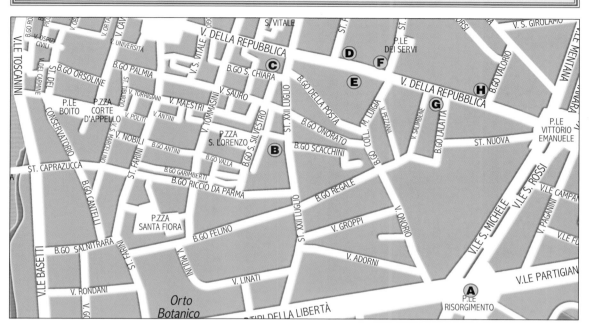

A) CASINÒ PETITOT

It owes its name to the famous court architect who designed it. It's located at the end of the *Stradone,* as *Via Martiri della Libertà* - the first example in Italy of French *Boulevards* - is commonly referred to in Parma. In fact it was the then prime minister *Du Tillot* who ordered the construction of both the *Stradone* and the *Casinò* entrusting their realization to *Petitot* in 1759. As it happens, they were both French. The ides was to endow the city with a place of leisure and a promenade, in what were then considered the outskirts of the city. The construction of this long way was thus decided. It's 740 meters long and 40 meters wide, with three lanes; the central one for coaches, the two lateral ones for pedestrians. At the end of it we find the Casinò, intended as a meeting place similar to the Parisian *Cafes.* The *Stradone* and the *Casinò* were inaugurated on June the 24th 1766.

93

B) CHURCH OF ST. QUENTIN

The first foundation of this Church dates as far back as the first years of the 9th century; it was rebuilt in the 12th century with a reverse orientation with respect to the current one; this may be deduced from the presence of a facade also in the back.

In 1560 the Benedictine Nuns had the Church completely rebuilt; they entrusted the design to *G. B. Fornovo*. The apse was added during a further restructuring carried out in the first years of 1800.

Internally there is a single nave, with four chapels per side.

M. A. Zucchi carved and inlayed the choir in 1515, on order by the Abbess *Giovanna Sanvitale*.

C) CHURCH OF ST CHRISTINE

The Church we see currently was built in 1650 on the ruins of a pre-existing temple dating back to the 10th century.

The facade was left uncompleted.

The inside is divided into three naves separated by Doric pilasters, with four chapels per side preceded by a small dome.

In the counter-facade, above the central portal, we find a wooden chancel of 1720. *Filippo Galletti* from Chieti frescoed the vaults and the domes.

D) DAZZI PALACE, FORMERLY CORRADI-CERVI

The architect *Domenico Cossetti*, a pupil of *Petitot*, built it between 1794 and 1797 on order by the marquis *Gian Francesco Corradi Cervi*. The facade is distinguished by two columns and two pilasters with Corinthian capitals, which start from the large balcony of the *piano nobile* and support a cornice and the tympanum entablature at third-floor height. An elegant balustrade composed of small columns surmounts the fourth floor. In the courtyard, on a large marble basin, a beautiful statue sculptured in 1832 by *Tommaso Bandini* portrays *Innocence*.

E) RANGONI FARNESE PALACE

Although still a property of the Rangoni family, in 1690 it became the residence of *Odoardo Farnese* and his wife *Dorotea*, just after their marriage. *Odoardo* entrusted its restoration to *Ferdinando Bibiena* for the brickwork and to *G. B. Barberini* for the internal and external stucco decorations. The long facade has two rows of windows, decorated with cornices and entablatures. The large portal is surmounted by the ducal coat of arms. It's enclosed between two big telamons supporting the balcony on the *piano nobile*.

It now accommodates the Prefecture, therefore only the atrium, the courtyard and the large stairway can be seen.

1: Church of St. Quentin - The former cloister
2: Church of St. Christine - The facade
3: Church of St. Christine - The inside
4: Dozzi Palace: the facade
5: Rangoni Farnese Palace - The entrance

F) CHURCH OF ST. ANTONIO ABATE

If was established in 1402 by the monks of St. Antonio, but in 1712 the Cardinal *Francesco Sanvitale* decided to reconstruct it, entrusting the design to *Ferdinando Bibiena,* the court scenographer. The construction was interrupted in 1714 because of the Cardinal's death, and was resumed only in 1759 under *Gaetano Ghidetti's* guidance. He strictly followed Bibiena's design, changing only some details. The marble facade is divided in three floors and includes a large triumphal arch. The inside has a single nave and four chapels per side, and is the triumph of the Baroque style. At first sight one does not realize being in a sacred place, also because of the impressive stagy effect created by the inlayed double vault. On the counter-facade above the portal there's beautiful wooden chancel. 1st right Chapel: above the altar there's a canvas painted by *Giovanni Gottardi* in 1765 depicting *St. Peter healing a cripple.* 2nd right Chapel: *Gian Bettino Cignaroli* painted in 1766 *The escape to Egypt,* a canvas placed above the altar. Presbytery: the altar is a work by Ghidetti, while *Alessandro Bartoli* carried out the balustrade. The author of the choir is *Domenico Chierici.* On the bottom wall, the large fresco depicting the *Apparition of Christ to St. Antonio* was painted by *Giuseppe Pieroni,* who is also the author of the frescoes that can be seen on the vaults though the fretwork: *The glory of St. Antonio* in the central one; *Angels and Saints* in the other ones. Along the two walls of the nave, large niches accommodate a series of statues by *C. Callani* known as *of the Beatitudes.*

2nd left Chapel: *Pompeo Batoni* painted in 1777 the altarpiece depicting *The predication of the Baptist.*

1st left Chapel: above the altar a large canvas painted in 1766 by *G. Pieroni* portrays *the Crucifixion.*

1

2

Church of St. Antonio Abate
1: The facade
2: The fretwork double vault
3: The statues of the Beatitudes
4: Marchi Palace, the seat of the Institute of
   Verdi Studies

G) MARCHI PALACE

It's one of the city's most important palaces. The Abbot architect *Giovanni Furlani* built it between 1770 and 1774 on commission by the marquis *Scipione Grillo*. The smooth rustic work facade is divided in three floors separated by white stucco cornices.

The windows of the ground floor and of the *piano nobile* are decorated with white pilasters supporting tympanums that are alternatively curvilinear and triangular. The top floor ones are a lot simpler.

The sumptuous portal is sided by two Doric columns supporting the large balcony on the first floor.

Two large courtyards are inside:
the first one has a portico supported by Doric columns, while the second one encloses a garden.

The stairway that bifurcates after the first flight of stairs is really fine, with its marble balustrade and the statues on the walls.

H) CHURCH OF THE HOLY SEPULCHRE

This Gothic style construction was built in 1257 on a pre-existing temple dating back to the year 1100. *Bartolomeo Predasoli* carried out the Renaissance facade we can see currently at the beginning of '500.

Simone Moschino designed the Baroque bell tower built in 1616. In 1780 the right side was redone in Neo-classic style on a design by *Antonio Brianti.* **The inside** with its single nave and Gothic arcades has five Chapels per side, and two beside the presbytery. The coffered ceiling is extremely refined. *Lorenzo Zaniboni* and *Gioacomo Trioli* carved and inlayed the coffers in the first years of '600.

Lionello Spada frescoed the walls above the arcades with portraits of Saints at the beginning of '600.

1st right Chapel: above the altar a large polyptych attributed to *Alessandro Araldi* portrays in its upper part *The Deposition*, and its lower one *Angels and Saints.*

The bronze Baptismal font by *Emilio Trombara* is a fine work of art.

2nd right Chapel: the altarpiece painted in 1621 by *Pier Antonio Barnabei* portrays *The Virgin with Child and Four Saints.*

3rd right Chapel: it has a lateral exit and no important decorations.

4th right Chapel: above the altar, a beautiful canvas painted in 1754 by *Gian Bettino Cignaroli* portrays the *Guardian Angel*.

5th right Chapel: it accommodates a beautiful 18th-century wooden chancel.

6th right Chapel: *Giulio Cesare Amidano* painted the large canvas depicting *Jesus dead*.

Presbytery: *Cesare Baglioni* frescoed the vaults and the lunettes in the first years of '700 with scenes from the New Testament, while the apsidal bowl-shaped vault and the walls were painted by *Ferdinando Bibiena*.

Above the Baroque altar a large altarpiece portrays *The Resurrection. Francesco Monti* painted it in 1670.

6th left Chapel: frescoes and furniture were carried out in 1465.

5th left Chapel: it accommodates a beautiful 16th-century organ.

4th left Chapel: *Sebastiano Galeotti* painted in 1723 the large canvas above the altar depicting *The mystical marriage of St. Catherine*.

3rd left Chapel: a luxurious Baroque niche encloses a wooden statue of *Our Lady of Sorrows*.

2nd left Chapel: above the altar a beautiful canvas by *Alessandro Mori* portrays *Jesus*

between the Saints Sebastian and Rocco with a landscape of Parma on the background.

1st left Chapel: *Cesare Baglioni* frescoed the vaults and the walls.

In the centre, a copy by Alessandro Mori of *Correggio's* famous *Madonna of the bowl*. The original is stored in the National Gallery. There are many paintings also in the atrium to the sacristy, and in the sacristy itself: among them we would like to mention a canvas painted in 1550 by *Girolamo Mazzola Bedoli* depicting *Our Lady, Jesus, St. John and Saints*.

The fine Renaissance cloister built between 1493 and 1495 by *Ziliolo da Reggio* is enclosed in a beautiful portico, with columns and capitals sculptured by *Antonio Ferrari d'Agrate*.

1: Church of the Holy Sepulchre - The facade
2: Church of the Holy Sepulchre - The inside
3: Viale Toschi - E. Ximenes (1931): Monument to Victory
4: Piazza della Stazione - Monument to V. Bottego
Page 100-100. Night view of the city

This itinerary includes the whole of the Northern area, including the Via Aemilia and the course of the Po river. We shall begin informally from the small village that gave birth to _Giuseppe Verdi,_ as homage to the great Maestro.

A) RONCOLE VERDI

Giuseppe Verdi was born in a farmhouse of this small Busseto hamlet on October the 10th 1813. The native house was declared a national monument just after the Maestro's death, which occurred in Milan on January the 27th 1901. The medieval *Church of St, Michael* rises just by the house, and it was here that the young Verdi started to play the 18th-century organ that can still be seen. His birth certificate is stored in the bell tower. Many paintings and frescoes spanning from the 14th to the 18th century can be admired in the Church.

The *Verdianeum* has been held in the square every year since 1985. It's a summer opera event dedicated to Verdi's immortal music. The square is dedicated to *Giovanni Guareschi* because he lived his last years here creating his popular characters *Peppone and Don Camillo.*

1: *Verdi's portrait carried out by G. Boldini in 1886*
2: *Roncole Verdi: The Maestro's native house*
3: *Roncole - Giuseppe Verdi birth certificate, kept in the bell tower of the Church of San Michele*

1

2

3

Roncole Verdi - Church of St. Michael
1: The Church of St.. Michael
2: The organ
3: The font where Verdi was baptised
4: A chapel with the 15th century frescoes
5: The keyboard of the organ played by Verdi

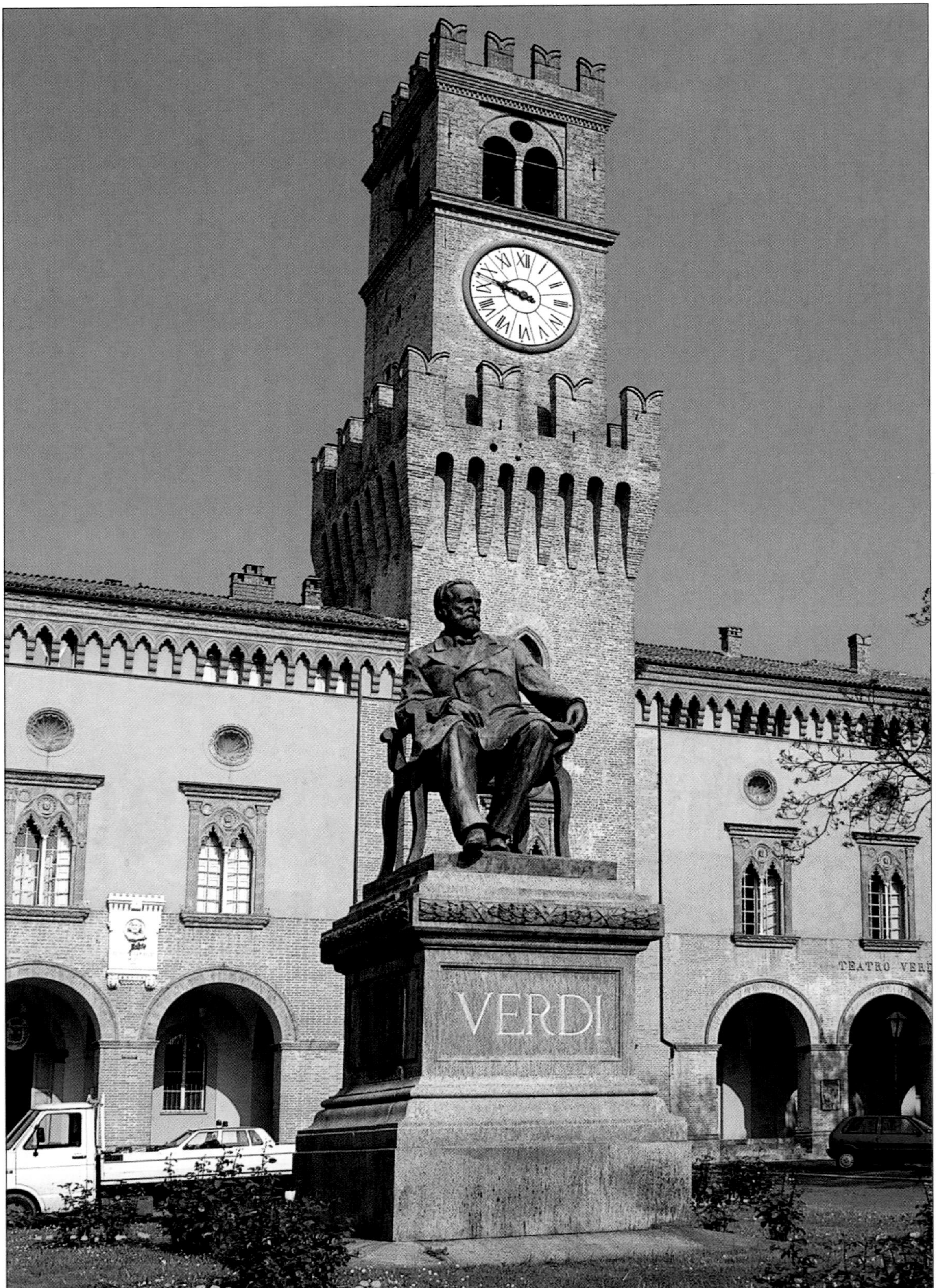

1

B) BUSSETO

It's the village where Verdi moved when he was 10 years old in order to be able to attend the grammar school.

Here *Antonio Barezzi,* a rich trader that was a friend of Verdi's father, immediately recognized the youngster's astounding talent and sent him to study with *Ferdinando Provesi,* the director of the Music School and organist in the Cathedral of Parma. In 1828, when Verdi was only 15 years old, the city orchestra played a concert with the music he composed.

In those years Verdi could further improve his musical vocation by frequently visiting Barezzi's house, where a grand piano was made available to him.

Verdi fell in love with Barezzi's daughter, *Margherita,* whom he married on May the 4th 1836, after having won the competitive examination for a post as Music teacher for the Municipality of Parma.

Although it can boast more ancient origins, the history of Busseto begins with that of *Oberto Pallavicino.* In 1249 he was named Imperial Vicar for the area spanning from the Po river to the Apennines and from the Taro to the Chiavenna, with Busseto as capital. In 1533 the town was appointed *City* of the Emperor *Charles V,* on the occasion of his visit to meet *Girolamo Pallavicino.*

1: *Rocca Pallavicino with monument to Giuseppe Verdi*
2: *Via Roma*
3: *The old palace of the Commune*

In 1587 it was conquered by the *Farnese*, who had become the Dukes of Parma and Piacenza since 1545. The *Old Palace of the Commune* dating back to the 15th century, and the *Pallavicino Fortress* dating back to the 13th, face the central square, named after the Maestro.

The fort was restored in the second half of 1800, especially to accommodate the *Verdi Theatre,* which was inaugurated on August the 15th 1868.

1: The Pallavicino Fortress
2: The G. Verdi Theatre
3: Barezzi House: The piano played by Verdi

1

The Collegiate Church of St. Bartholomew also faces the square. It's a fine Gothic style Church dating back to the first half of the 15th century.

On the facade, beside the central portal surmounted by a beautiful rosette, a memorial stone written in Latin recalls the meeting between the emperor *Charles V* and the Pope *Paolo III Farnese* in 1543.

The inside, with three naves, was restored in Rococo style in 1700 and contains many works of art. We would like to recall: *Mary Immaculate and Saints,* a 16th-century work by *Andrea Mainardi,* a 15th-century wooden Crucifix, and the altar piece depicting *The Assumption of Mary,* painted by *G. E. Draghi.*

The *Oratory of the Holy Trinity* dating back to the 12th century is very interesting.

The inside with a single nave stores the remains of the *Blessed Rolando de' Medici* since 1380.

The altarpiece is a fine work of art. It depicts *The Trinity and the Saints Apollonia and Lucy at the sides of the Cross*, and was painted in 1575 by *Vincenzo Campi.*

The wedding between Giuseppe Verdi and Margherita Barezzi took place just in this Oratory in 1836.

Relics of Verdi can be seen in Barezzi Palace, now the seat of the *Associazione Amici di Verdi,* which in 1979 financed and took care of the restoration.

Other relics of Verdi and over 30,000 volumes are stored in the Library established in 1768 by *Ferdinand of Bourbon.*

Just outside the town it's possible to visit the *Civic Museum* accommodated in *Villa Pallavicino.* It's a building with five bodies arranged as a checkerboard built in the 16th century, and surrounded by a ditch. All the interiors are frescoed and decorated with stuccoes.

Many concerts are held yearly in Busseto, among which the important *International Contest for Verdi voices.*

Busseto
1: The Collegiate Church of St. Bartholomew
2: The Oratory of the Holy Trinity where
*   Verdi got married in 1836.*

2

C) S. AGATA, VILLA VERDI

Verdi purchased this villa surrounded by a magnificent garden and a large estate in 1848. He personally took care of the restoration and the extensions on the sides and the back.

The heirs of the Maestro still live in the upper floors, but it's possible to visit the rooms on the ground floor, which belonged to Verdi and *Giuseppina Strepponi,* a singer with whom Verdi fell in love after the untimely death of his first wife. It's possible to see many objects that were part of the Maestro's life, among which the spinet he used to compose some of his most famous operas.

1: The villa
2: The red living room

1

D) SORAGNA

In 1198 Soragna became a feud of *Guido Lupi,* a descendant of the Lombard house of the *Obertenghi.* Previously it had been a property of the Church, and then of the Pallavicino.

The *Fortress* is still a property of the *Meli Lupi* family, which lives in it. It had been built as a fortress in the 14th century, but in the following centuries it was changed into a residence.

It has a square shape, and the corners have bastions that are typical of the fortress; it can be accessed by crossing the ditch on the brickwork bridge that has replaced the pre-existing drawbridge since the 17th century. The park is really beautiful. Two isles in a little lake are dedicated to *Eros* and *Jupiter.* The inside is rich with galleries and halls, all of them richly frescoed both on the vaults

Meli Lupi Palace
1: The entrance from the city square
2: A wing of the palace and the garden
3: The facade and the main entrance
4: The stairway

2

3

4

and on the walls, and decorated with tapestries (the one made with mother of pearl depicting the *Garden of Eden* is really beautiful), paintings, furniture and mirrors.

The *Armoury* stores a rich collection of halberds, pistols, arquebuses and even a small cannon.

The fortress accommodated also the Emperor *Charles V,* and one of the frescoes by the *Bibiena* brothers dedicated to the history of the Meli Lupi family recalls the dinner held in his honour. The *Chapel of the Holy Cross* inside the fortress is beautiful, rich with works of art. A visit should be paid also to the *Synagogue* dating back to the 16th century - now a museum - and the *Church of St. James,* from the second half of the 18th century.

Meli Lupi Palace - The open gallery

E) FONTANELLATO

The town's name comes from *Fontana lata* (big fountain) for the abundance of water that distinguishes the area. The city is developed around the powerful *Sanvitale Fortress,* whose origins date back to the 10th century. The current structure, although modified in the 17th century on a design by *Smeraldo Smeraldi,* dates back to the 14th century, when the area became a feud of the *Sanvitale* family who decided to make the fortress its residence.

The majestic building surrounded by a large ditch has a square base, and three cylindrical towers on three corners and a square one on the fourth one.

It may be accessed by crossing a bridge and passing under the arch of the *Mastio,* whose vault is frescoed with the coats of arms of the families allied of the Sanvitale.

One then reaches the courtyard, which is surrounded by halls accommodating an out and out art gallery with many portraits of the components of the Sanvitale, Farnese and Bourbon families.

Since 1948, when the fortress became a property of the Municipality, these halls constitute the *Town Museum.*

On the ground floor we also find the *Small Hall of Parmigianino,* commonly known as *Paola Gonzaga's* - Galeazzo Sanvitale's wife - *boudoir.* It's a small rectangular room frescoed by the great artist when he was only a little more than twenty years old.

The vault depicts the sky surrounded by a rose hedge, with a large gilded rosette in the middle enclosing a mirror.

The walls, subdivided at the summits in 14 lunettes, are frescoed with scenes from the legend of *Diana and Actaeon*, taken from Ovid's Metamorphosis.

The various scenes describe the tragedy of Actaeon who, while hunting, came upon Diana and her maidservants taking a bath naked in a lake.

The goddess changed him into a stag and had him tore to pieces by her dogs, for the mere reason of having seen her unclothed. One of the shortest walls portrays Paola Gonzaga herself in a meditative attitude.

1: Fortress of Sanvitale - Aerial view
2: The coats of arms of the families allied of the Sanvitale frescoed on the large vault of the Mastio

In creating the whole of the decorations Parmigianino was undoubtedly inspired by seeing *Correggio's* Hall of St. Paul, also for the bamboo canes running from the vaults to the summits of the lunettes.

On the first floor there are many other halls, among which we would like to mention the *Armoury* for the rich collection of ancient weapons, and the *Gallery of Portraits* which displays the portraits of all the components of the Sanvitale Family subdivided in three series. It starts with the founder of the family, *Ugo,* who lived in the 12th century, up to the count *Giovanni*, who sold the fortress to the municipality in 1951 before his death.

Entering the village coming from Parma we find the *Sanctuary of the Blessed Virgin of the Rosary.* It was built in the 17th century

and reconstructed various times in the following centuries.

A tabernacle placed on the high altar encloses the miraculous wooden statue of the *Virgin with Child*, both of them crowned and richly dressed. An unknown artist realized it in 1615. The first miracle occurred in 1628 with the sudden recovery of a dying child. Since then many miracles have been attributed to the Virgin, and the Church has the walls covered with invoking or thanksgiving votive offerings.

Fortress of Sanvitale
1: The courtyard
2-3: Details of the hall of Parmigianino
4: Fortress of Sanvitale: The armoury

5: Sanctuary of the B.V. of the Rosary: the facade
6: The tabernacle with the miraculous statue

F) S. SECONDO

The origins of this beautiful village date back to the 9th century, Since the beginning of 1200 until 1802 it was a feud of the *Rossi* family, which is responsible for the construction of the Castle. *Pier Maria detto il Magnifico* began the works in 1438. He ruled the marquesate until 1482, when he died defeated by *Ludovico il Moro.* The latter put the castle to fire and sword, grievously damaging it.

It was rebuilt starting from 1505 *by Troilo I,* which had been reintegrated in the marquesate and named Senator of Milan by the King of France, *Luis XII.* He carried out the construction and changed the building from a fortress into a gentlemanly dwelling, creating the honour courtyard surrounded by porticoes and loggias. In the second half of 1800 the castle was demolished for the

San Secondo
1: The Mastio
2: The Castle
3: Hall of annals - The battle of S. Donino

most part, and only the Mastio and a wing are left.

On the first floor there are many halls, all frescoed during the 16th century, among which we mention: *The hall of the golden donkey*, which owes its name to the scenes depicted on the walls and the vault taken from Apuleius' novel bearing the same name. *Matteo Maria Boiardo* had translated it in that period;

The hall of the fall of giants, whose frescoes portray just the scenes from their myth and other mythological episodes;

The hall of annals, so called because starting from the right of the monumental and fine fireplace there are frescoes depicting scenes portraying the annals of the Rossi family. The frescoes on the vault deal with the same theme.

The *Oratory of the enclosure* should also be remembered. *Ferdinando Bibiena* and *Sebastiano Ricci* richly frescoed and decorated it in the late '600, on commission by the count *Scipione Rossi*.

The ceiling of the Hall of the golden donkey with the scenes from Apuleius' novel

G) FONTEVIVO

It's worth a visit to see The *Cistercian Abbey*, whose construction began in 1142 and went on for almost two centuries. Unfortunately many restorations performed without sufficient care have slightly spoilt both the Gothic style facade and the inside. A small statue portraying a *Madonna with Child* and dating back to the 13th century has been recently restored. The author is believed to be *Benedetto Antelami*.

Cistercian Abbey
1: The facade
2: The statue of the Madonna with Child attributed to B. Antelami (13th cent.)
3: The inside

H) COLORNO

The small town is located on the confluence of the Lorno stream in the Parma, and this is where the name comes from: in fact, the Roman settlement was called *Caput Lurni*.

The construction of the fortress began in the 10th century. *Roberto Sanseverino* changed it into a gentlemanly residence in the 15th century. He was related to Milan's Sforza family, and had been invested with the feud in 1458. The rule of the Sanseverino ended in 1611, when *Ranuccio I Farnese* condemned *Barabara Sanseverino* and some of her relatives to death accusing them of plotting against him. He annexed the feud to the Duchy of Parma and Piacenza.

In 1663 *Ranuccio II* decided to turn the castle into a summer residence for him and the whole court.

The restoration and the extension continued with *Francesco,* the last of the house, who entrusted the direction of the works to *Ferdinando Bibiena,* the court scenographer.

The current appearance of the sumptuous building is just the one given to it by *Bibiena*. He worked to it between 1712 and 1727, also rearranging the park - which he enriched with statues, fountains and gardens, to the extent that the palace of Colorno is called the *small Versailles.*

In 1732 the Duchy's rule passed on from the Farnese to the Bourbons, in the person of *Don Charles,* the son of Elisabetta Farnese and Philip V.

In 1734 Charles moved to Naples, which he had in the meantime conquered, and to make the new court more luxurious he completely stripped those of Parma and Colorno. The brother *Philip*, duke since 1749, took care of the palace re-furnishing and changed the interiors, entrusting the court architect *Petitot* with the task.

Ducal Palace

In the following century *Marie Louise* carried out further changes, especially in the park that was changed into an English garden.

With the upcoming of the Kingdom of Italy and the subsequent end of the Duchy, the palace fell into abandonment and the *Savoia* moved all the furnishings and collections to their residences.

Lately the palace has been restored and opened to the public, who can now admire its richness.

Nearby the park it's possible to visit the *Aranciaia,* a construction built by Bibiena to place the citrus plants to winter rest. It's now the seat of the *Farming Civilization Museum.*

A visit should be paid also to the *Church of*

St. Liborio. It was built on a design by the architect *Petitot,* and ordered by the devoted Philip, who used it as *Ducal Chapel.* The Neo-classic facade is decorated with statues by *Gaetano Cignaroli.*
There are many frescoes and fine stuccoes inside. Among the many works of art we would like to remember the polychrome marble floor in the presbytery, the statue of

St. Liborio by *Gaetano Callani* placed in a large carved-wood niche, the organ sound boxes and the chancels by the Flemish *Ignatius Verstrackt,* the choir and the lectern by

1: Spectacular view of the Ducal Palace
2: The internal courtyard
3: The stairway of honour
4: The park and the back of the palace

1

the French *M. Poncet,* and the organ built in 1792 by the *Serassi brothers.* The latter is used during the *Yearly review of organ music.*

The *Cistercian Charterhouse of Paradigna* also deserves a visit. It's located on the state road between Colorno and Parma.

It's a severe building erected in the first years of the 14th century by the Cistercian Monks. It inspired *Stendhal* for his famous novel *The Charterhouse of Parma.*

The extremely sober facade was rebuilt in the first years of '700.

The inside is divided in three naves with cross-vaults, separated by bundle-columns with stone capitals.

1: Ducal Palace - A hall

Church of St. Liborio
2: The nave
3: The organ by the Serassi Brothers
4: The choir (detail)

I) SISSA

The village's name comes from the fact that in ancient times, when the village was included in the territory of *Palasone*, it was separated (in Italian, *scisso*) from the rest of the town following the flooding of the river

Taro. Although its origins are older, the history of Sissa begins in 1362 when *Gherardo Terzi* asked *Bernabò Visconti*, then the lord of the territory, for a ruined tower on the shores of the Po river. It's almost certainly the *Torricella*, now a crossroad of the Po tourism because a nice river port was built in the area. It may be reached after having crossed the beautiful park called *Meadows of Marie Louise*. Once it had obtained the rule on the area, the *Terzi* family had the powerful *Fortress* built around the mid-15th century, whose majestic tower is still standing. Extended in 1700 to make it a gentlemanly residence, it's now the seat of the City Council. Sissa's *Parish Church of Our Lady of The Assumption* is also worth a visit. It is of Romanesque origins, but it was completely rebuilt in the 19th century. A 15th-century fresco dedicated to *Our Lady of Graces* may be admired in it.

L) ROCCABIANCA

The name of the village located between the Po, Taro and Stirone rivers comes from that of *Bianca Pellegrini, Pier Maria Rossi's* lover, who donated her the *Fortress* that he had built for her around the mid-15th century. Notwithstanding the many changes it underwent, the fortress is still imposing. The remains of a cycle of frescoes dedicated to the *Stories of Griselda* taken from *Boccaccio*'s *Decameron* may be admired in the internal halls. In the village there's the beautiful *Church of the Saints Bartholomew and Michael,* which dates back to the 16th century. Nature lovers shouldn't miss a visit to the shores of the Po river, where century-old poplars can be admired.

In the nearby small hamlet of *Fontanelle* it's possible to visit the native house of *Giovanni Guareschi*, where a documentation concerning the author of the characters *Don Camillo and Peppone* has been arranged.

1: Sissa: the Fortress
2: Roccabianca - The entrance to the fortress

M) ZIBELLO

Connected for religious reasons to the nearby Cremona, starting from 1249 the village became a feud of the marquis *Uberto Pallavicino*, who received the investiture from the emperor *Frederick II*. The Pallavicino dominated the territory until the beginning of '800, and they are responsible for the most important monuments realized between the late 15th and the early 16th century:

The Old Palace facing the village square; the *Church of the Sts. Jarvis and Protaso;* the former *Dominican Monastery* that currently accommodates the *G. Riccardi Museum of farming civilization*. Beside agricultural tools fishing equipment is also on display in the *Secrets of the PO river* section. Zibello is the place of origin of the notorious *culatello*, which gourmets consider the *king of charcuterie*. The Commission for the protection of Zibello's *culatello* has been granted the use of the *DOP* (denomination of protected origin) mark by the European Union, because this typical product is still produced with the craftsmanship methods used in the past centuries, when the Pallavicino gave it as a present to their most illustrious guests. It's the pork's buttock tied in the shape of a pear. It has found in the humus of this land the ideal climate for its maturation and preservation.

The *Festival of the culatello* is held in June, every year.

1: Pallavicino Palace
2: The Church of the Saints Jarvis and Protaso.

1

A) SALSOMAGGIORE

This beautiful town located at the feet of the Parmesan Apennine at a height above sea level of 160 mt. Was already well known in Roman times for its salted waters spontaneously emerging from the ground.

After the emperor Charlemagne had granted its exploitation to some residents, the property of the territory passed first to the Pallavicino, then to the Farnese and the Bourbons, and finally to Marie Louise, who in 1847 allowed *Lodovico Rocca di Parma* to exploit the waters for therapeutic use.

Doctor *Lorenzo Berbieri*, the first one to discover the curative properties of the waters, started the transformation of the area from rural village to thermal bath resort, taking the example of the other European *Villes d'eaux*, using to a large extent the then flourishing *Art Nouveau* style. The large *Terme Berzieri* thermal baths have been dedicated to him. They were inaugurated in 1923 in pure *Art Deco style*, on a design by the architects Giusti and Bernardini, and decorations carried out by Galileo Ghini. In the meantime, the *Grand Hotel des Thermes* had already been built in the beginning of 1900, once again in Art Nouveau style. Today it's the Palace of Congresses. Boulevards and parks were built, and Salsomaggiore thus became an elegant garden town where to restore the body, with cures, and the spirit, with contact with nature and by participating to the countless cultural and mundane activities held there. Among these we would like to recall: the *Salso Film e TV Festival*, the final to elect *Miss Italy*, the *bridge* championships and the *checks* tournament.

1: The Berzieri Baths
2: The splendid Art Nouveau of an interior
3: The small lake

1

2

B) TABIANO

This delightful village plunged in the green-ery is located about 4 km. away from Salso-maggiore. Its life revolves around the large thermal baths dedicated to *Prof. Emilio Respighi* who co-operated with *Dr. Berzieri* and experimented and classified the cura-tive properties of the sulphuric waters of Tabiano.

B) PELLEGRINO PARMENSE

It's placed at 410 mt. above sea level on the state road no. 359. It was a feud of the Pal-lavicino, of the Fogliano and of the Meli Lupi. In the old town it's possible to admire the monastery founded by *St. Bernardino di Siena.* There are two other beautiful monu-ments: the 12th-century Castle and the *Sanctuary of the Madonna of Careno,* built in the 10th century and restructured in the 14th.

D) VARANO DE MELEGARI

The village is placed at the feet of the Apennines, and is dominated by the imposing massive structure of the Castle, which was built in 1208 on a pre-existing 11th-century fort. It was a feud of the Pallavicino family until 1782.

In the surroundings it's possible to visit the 15th-century *Church of St. Martin* and *Viezzano,* an ancient Medieval town with small cobbled streets enclosed in ancient stone houses and tower houses.

1: Tabiano - The Castle
2: Tabiano - A corner of the thermal park
3: Varano de Melegari - The Fortress
4: Pellegrino Parmense - The Parish Church

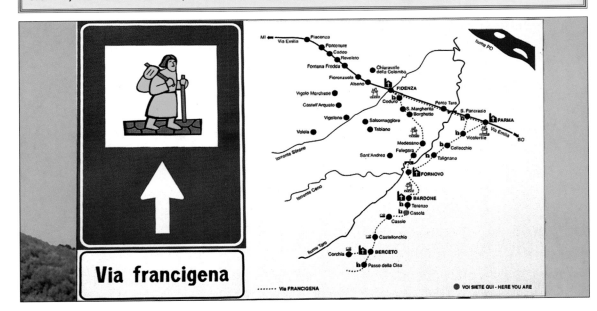

THE VIA FRANCIGENA

After Rome had become the centre of Christianity, al the roads that reached it where called *Romee.*

In the Middle Ages, the branch of the road to Rome that started off from *Canterbury,* off the gates of London, started to be called *Francigena,* or *Francesca.*

This name identified the road that was then starting to connect Italy with the countries over the Alps.

A very important testimony of these trips is the diary left by the Archbishop of Canterbury, *Sinergico,* which travelled to Rome in 990.

In Parmesan territory the Via Francigena was also called *way of the Mount Bardone* because the current *Passo della Cisa* was then called *Monte Bardone.*

The name comes from *Mons Longobardorum* (Mount of the Lombards), because this was the only way that reached the sea in Lunigiana from the Lombard capital, Pavia.

The main route starts in Fidenza and reaches the Cisa passing through Fornovo, Bordone and Berceto, touching other places with various detours.

An improvement route started from Fiorenzuola, in the nearby province of Piacenza, reached Bardi and Borgo Val di Taro in the Parmesan territory and then got reconnected with the Via Francigena in Lunigiana, crossing the *Passo del Bratello.*

A second improvement route started in Parma after having reached Castel Guelfo, Ponte Taro, and S. Pancrazio, because many pilgrims wanted to see the city that in those times received them in the Church of the Holy Cross.

The branch starting in Parma is reconnected with the main route in Fornovo through Vicofertile, Collecchio and Talignano.

In order to be able to restore and protect the pilgrims, hostels and hospitals were built near the main Cathedrals.

In the Parmesan territory they were for the most part in Romanesque style, therefore the various ways are also called *Romanesque Itineraries.*

The Via Francigena is now the foundation of a project by the *European Union,* which has declare it a *European Cultural Itinerary* as cultural, historic and artistic heritage of the new United Europe.

1) FIDENZA

It was founded at the end of the 2nd century BC with the name of *Fidentia:* the purpose was to create a bulwark to defend the passage on the nearby *Stirone* stream. Later on it was called *Borgo S. Donnino* because it was here that the Saint suffered the Martyrdom of beheading in 293 AD. Centuries later, when his remains were found, a small Parish Church was built in his honour because his remains were believed to be thaumaturgical. Later, it became the current Cathedral. The extension works began in the 12th century, but were interrupted and resumed only at the beginning of the 13th under the guidance of *Benedetto Antelami.* He sculptured the architrave surmounting the central portal with *scenes from the Martyrdom of St. Donnino,* the statues of *David and Ezekiel* placed on the sides of the portal, the lions supporting the pilasters of the arch before the portal, the architraves of the two lateral portals and the *Madonna on Throne with Child.* The latter is kept in the crypt, where the remains of the Saint are preserved in an Ark.

The thaumaturge Saint's fame and a miracle of the loaves performed by *St. Francesco* in 1215 while he had come to worship St. Donnino made Fidenza famous, making it one of the compulsory stops for the pilgrims that were going to Rome since the 1300 Jubilee.

The Cathedral is built in Lombard Romanesque style with Provençal influences, and is one of the few with a bell tower on each side of the facade.

Other monuments deserving a visit in Fidenza are:

Fidenza - The Cathedral
1: *The apsidal area*
2: *The splendid decorations on the right of the central portal*
3: *The central nave*
4: *The crypt*

The Church of St. Antonio Abate, built at the beginning of the 13th century in Romanesque style yet with a slight lean towards the rising Gothic style. It included a monastery and a hospital for the pilgrims.

The *Oratory of the Zeppella*, where St. Francesco performed the miracle.

The *Communal Palace*, built in Gothic Style between 1270 and 1354, and provided with the tower only in 1570.

The *City Theatre*, finished in 1861 on Nicola Bettoli's design.

Placed halfway between Parma and Piacenza, Fidenza still shows many signs of the Farnese's and Bourbons' rule.

Fidenza
1: The Cathedral - The facade
2: The Cathedral - The architrave of the central portal with scenes of St. Donnino's Martyrdom
3: The City Theatre
4: The Communal Palace

2) FORNOVO

It's an active village at the feet of the Apennines.

It was therefore a compulsory stop for the pilgrims, before confronting the impervious paths of the Mount Bardone.

Shelters and curing places for the travellers were built here, around the 13th-century Romanesque Parish dedicated to *St, Mary of the Assumption.*

The figure of a pilgrim is sculptured on the facade of the Parish, with the pannier on his back and five keys on his belt representing the five Roman Basilicas that where his destination.

The low-relieves decorating the facade and the sides are also beautiful.

In the very sober inside the depiction of the *Martyrdom of St. Mary of Antioch* stands out on the bottom wall. She is the protector of virgins and women in labour.

Fornovo - The Cathedral
1: The Pilgrim
2: Low relief on the left corner
3: The facade

3) OZZANO TARO: MUSEUM OF TIME AND OF FARMING CIVILIZATION

An old *farmhouse* of this hamlet placed halfway between Fornovo and Collecchio accommodates this enchanting museum, which is pointed out by a simple road sign. *Ettore Guatelli,* a poet and primary school teacher, created it with his passionate work dedicating to this collection all his leisure time and most of his working life earnings.

A son and brother of farmers, he never forgot his origins even when he had become a teacher, in fact he kept a diary on life in the fields. In the years immediately following the war, when mechanization was starting to prevail on the traditional working systems by hand, he realized that the objects and tools that had accompanied everyday working life in the fields for generations were soon to disappear.

Also inspired by the finding of an old worn-out boot with a patched upper shoe, he started to gather the objects that are now displayed in the museum.

In the beginning he was also helped by a bookseller who, besides books, sold old objects in his shop.

Moreover, he started to recover old thrown away things in dumps, and to visit farmhouses and old villages looking for old commodities that had been a part of that world's everyday life.

Once he realized he had gathered a large number of objects and tools, he decided to establish the Museum.

Helped by his pupils and friends he started to reorder and catalogue all the various findings, so that now the collection is fascinating not only for its peculiarity but also for the care and the method with which the findings have been displayed, creating out and out frescoes on the walls and ceilings.

Scissors, knives, hammers, shifting spanners, screw drivers, scalpels, axes, spades and hoes are displayed in such a way that they look like paintings.

The gathering continues, and Mr. Guatelli's only concern is that when he will not be able to take care of it this priceless historical heritage - which is a reference also for scholars - shouldn't go lost. He hopes some public or private body to preserve and enrich this fascinating adventure of his.

4) TERENZO

A detour of the Cisa state road 62 leads to this small village located at the feet of a wooded crag.

The bell tower of the beautiful Church dedicated to *Mary and St. Steven Protomartyr* located in the lower part of the village still stores a bell dating back to 1365, which warned the pilgrims about the existence of the cult and hospitality place.

1: Terenzio - The Church of Mary and St, Steven Protomartyr Bardone
2: The inside with the Romanesque altar
3: The Romanesque Parish

5) BARDONE

From Terenzo, continuing on a mountain road running amongst green fields full of colourful flowers, one reaches this small hamlet where the ancient Romanesque Parish stands out. It's rich with sculptures of those times, among which a precious sculptured-stone altar.

The Parish and the village were the last stop before confronting the path that led to Lunigiana, and still are a real oasis of tranquillity.

6) CASOLA

Going up on the state road 62 and continuing towards the Cisa it's possible to visit the *Church of St. Apollinare*, placed in the centre of this fine Medieval village.

7) CASSIO

From this beautiful Medieval village one can admire the *Devil's step faults,* a powerful cinder-colour rocky mass scattered with pinnacles, placed transversally across the valley.

8) CASTELLONCHIO

It owes its name to the presence of a castle built in the 12th century by the Commune of Parma as a checkpoint of the path to Lunigiana.

Medieval streets and buildings can be admired here.

9) CORCHIA

Moving along a pleasant detour from Berceto it's possible to visit this pleasant medieval village that has stopped in time thanks to its isolated position.

Among the stone houses the stone Parish and bell tower stand out.

It really is a plunge into the past.

1: Cassio - The Parish Church
2: Corchia - The ancient Parish Church

10) BERCETO

By detouring from the state road 62 one reaches this beautiful village plunged in the woods. It was built around the 8th-century Benedictine Abbey built by the Lombard king *Liutprand.* The Bishop of Rennes, *Moderanno,* was *one* of the Abbots. He still is the Patron Saint of the village. The lunette and the architrave of the central portal dating back to the 12th century depict scenes from *The Passion of Christ and the Crucifixion.*

In the adjacent *Chapel of St. Apollonia* it's possible to admire the treasure of the sacred furnishings, among which a glass chalice dating back to the 10th century stands out.

The ruins of the *Castle of the Counts Rossi* are also interesting.

The village is equipped with modern receptive structures inserted in the quiet medieval atmosphere that can be felt in the whole centre of the village, walking on paved streets sided by old stone buildings. It is advisable to visit one of the local restaurants to taste the delicious dishes based on pore mushrooms, unanimously recognized as the best ones of the whole Apennines.

11) PASSO DELLA CISA

It's the border between Emilia and Liguria. Nothing is left of the ancient structures, and a fine little church was built in 1910 on the highest peak. It may be reached by going up a long stairway.

A beautiful scenery of Lunigiana may be enjoyed form the parvis, and in the brightest days it's even possible to see the sea.

1: The ruins of the Castle of the Counts Rossi
2: The Cathedral - The lunette and the architrave
3: The Cathedral - The facade
4: Passo della Cisa

A view of the Apennines with the bold motor way viaduct with overlapping lanes.

As we have said in the introduction, a detour of the Via Francigena started from Fiorenzuola, and more precisely from the ancient Cistercian Abbey of Chiaravalle della Colomba, a stop for the pilgrims. Being in Parmesan territory, we recommend carrying out the trip in the opposite direction, starting from Berceto and then turning down the state road 523, which will lead us to see castles and Parish Churches along the Taro valley.

1) BORGO VAL DI TARO

This large village was at first inhabited by the Ligurians and then conquered by the Romans in 160 BC.

The *Landi* family ruled it in the Middle Ages. It later passed under the domination of the Farnese and then the Bourbons, becoming a part of the Duchy.

The village's structure is typically modern but notable monuments are left, among which we would like to mention:

The Church of St. Antonino

the first foundation dates back to the 13th century, but *Ranuccio I Farnese* had it rebuilt in 1667.

The Latin-cross shaped inside contains a beautiful 15th-century wooden Crucifix and a fine organ built by the *Serassi* brothers.

The Church of St. Dominick

It dates back to the first half 15th century but it owes the current appearance to a restoration performed in 1674.

The inside is divided in three naves separated by stone columns. It contains beauti-

144

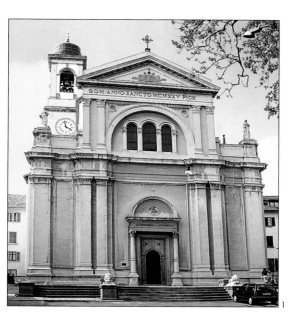

ful paintings, and a 1700 fresco in the sacristy.

Walking in the town centre it's possible to admire the beautiful decorations on *Boveri Palace*. They were carried out in honour of Elisabetta Farnese in 1714.

Borgo Val di Taro can also boast a gastronomic tradition consisting of pore mushrooms and game.

Borgo Val di Taro
1: The Church of St. Antonino
2: The Church of St. Dominick
3: Boveri Palace

2) COMPIANO

By making a short detour form the state road 523 it's possible to visit the splendid 15th-century castle, whose history is documented by a memorial stone on the boundary walls. The powerful polygonal-based building is built with towers and communication trenches on the side of an escarpment dominating the Taro valley.

3) BEDONIA

The village shows traces of the nearby Liguria, as the lightly coloured houses - so unusual for the Parmesan Apennine - prove. There are no ancient historical elements, although the place is mentioned in the Traian Table of the 2nd century AD as *Saltus Bituniae.* The town is dominated by the imposing mass of the *Sanctuary of the Madonna of St. Mark,* built in 1950 beside the imposing *Bishop Seminary* dating back to 1846. The latter accommodates the *ancient library,* the *Parmigiani Art Gallery,* with paintings of '600 and '700, the *Museum of Natural history* and the *planetarium.*

4) BARDI

The village's history is bound with that of the powerful castle dominating it.

After the void left by the fall of the Roman Empire, groups of Lombard warriors known as the *Arimanni* founded a village in the 7th century at the feet of the enormous red rock cliff on which the fortress rises, which they named Bardi.

The first news we have of the castle-fortress are dated 898, when, under the rule of *Berengarius I,* the Bishop of Piacenza *Everardo* bought half of the rock on which the fortress had been recently built. The purpose of this was to give shelter to the people of the area who were suffering incursions from *Hungarian* warriors. This is the reason for the castle's enormous dimensions.

1: Compiano - The Castle
2: Bedonia - The Sanctuary of the Madonna of St. Mark
3: Bardi - The imposing mass of the fortress on the overhanging rock

3

From the second half of the 13th century the area fell under the rule of the *Landi* family, which in 1551 managed to obtain the title of Marquisate from the emperor *Charles V*, together with the right to mint

coins. In those centuries the fortress was extended and consolidated, until the last of the Landi, *Filippo II,* decided to make it also a gentlemanly residence at the beginning of the 17th century. He had many halls frescoed, creating also a library and an art gallery.

In 1679 the castle became a property of the Farnese, and in 1764 of the Bourbons.

While visiting the castle it's possible to admire magnificent views from the communication trenches and the towers.

In the internal halls we find a notable quantity of medieval weapons and war machines, as well as the *Poaching museum.* The yearly *Tenzone di Bardi* is held on the third Sunday of July. It's an event with tournaments and dinners in medieval costumes.

In the village, the Parish Church dedicated to *The Blessed Virgin of Sorrows* accommodates an altarpiece by *Parmigianino* portraying *The mystical Wedding of St. Catherine.*

Bardi
1: The entrance of the fortress
2: The internal courtyard
3: View from a communication trench
4: One of the medieval war machines

Church of the Blessed Virgin of Sorrows
6: The facade
7: Parmigianino: The Mystical Wedding of St. Catherine

VIA FRANCIGENA - DETOUR B

1) VICOFERTILE • 2) TALIGNANO • 3) SALA BAGANZA • 4) TORRECHIARA • 5) MAGNANI-ROCCA FOUNDATION • 6) MONTECHIARUGOLO • MONTICELLI TERME

As we have said before, a second detour to the Via Francigena was the one covered by the pilgrims that had gone to Parma. Having already described the Church of the Holy Cross that was the destination of the pilgrims in the city, we shall start from here. Turning down on the state road 62 leading to Collecchio we can reach the Romanesque Parishes and the castles in the area located before the hills south of Parma.

1) VICOFERTILE

After about 4 km, a short detour on the right leads us to this small hamlet. In its centre it's possible to admire a small Romanesque Church dating back to the 12th century dedicated to *St. Geminiano*, which used to be one of the pilgrims' destinations. The facade, with a slightly splayed portal, and the sides are still the original ones, while the apsidal part and the Baroque bell tower were rebuilt in the 17th century.

In the sober interior it's possible to admire a baptismal font and six capitals, all of them sculptured in the 17th century. While the external part of the font bears relief figures officiating the sacrament of baptism, the capitals portray dancing animals, floral motifs and the expulsion of Adam and Eve from the Garden of Eden.

1: A view of the Parmesan Apennine

Vicofertile - Church of St. Geminiano
2: The facade
3: The inside
4: The 12th-century baptismal font

2) TALIGNANO

Continuing the trip on the state road 62, beyond Collecchio, a detour on the right leads us to this beautiful 12th-century Romanesque Parish. It's located on a crossroads between a branch of the Via Francigena, and plunged in the greenery of the woods.

3) SALA BAGANZA

Starting from Talignano and crossing the *Carrega meadows Regional Park* one reaches Sala Baganza, where it's possible to admire the *Fortress*. It was built in 1477 by *Gilberto III Sanvitale*, but it later passed on to the Farnese who made it one of their summer residences.

It owes its current appearance to modifications performed in '800.

On the first floor we can admire the magnificent frescoes in the *Chapel*, executed in 1569 by *Bernardino Campi.* He was certainly inspired by Correggio's *Hall of St. Paul,* and by the one by Parmigianino in the Fortress of Sanvitale, in Fontanellato.

There are indeed the same garlands of roses functioning as the background of Angels with the symbols of the Passion.

Other fine works of arts are the allegoric depictions of the Arts and Virtues, painted in 1727 by *Sebastiano Galeotti* on commission by Antonio Farnese to decorate the *Hall of Apotheosis.*

1: Talignano - The facade of the Parish
2: Talignano - The lunette depicting psychostasy
  (the weighing of souls)
3: Sala Baganza - The Fortress

4) TORRECHIARA

Going towards Langhirano one sees on the right the immense mass of the Castle, which may be reached by turning down on a short detour.

The one we see today was rebuilt between 1448 and 1460 for *Pier Maria Rossi,* lord of the area, on the summit of a hill.

It's fortified with a triple circle of walls and surrounded by the ancient town, which is enclosed in the outer one. It's one of the most notable examples of Renaissance building. It has a square base, with four corner towers. From the elegant courtyard of honour one goes up to the *piano nobile,* where it's possible to admire the *Golden Room. Benedetto Bembo* frescoed its vaults with the love story between *Pier Maria Rossi* and *Bianca Pellegrini* around 1450.

The artist made them the main characters of a chivalry novel, with Bianca visiting the beloved Pier Maria's 40 castles. It portrays also castles no longer existing nowadays, making the fresco also an important iconography document.

The walls are decorated with fired tiles that used to be gold-laminated; this is where the hall's name comes from.

The tiles bear the coat of arms of the Rossi and the initials of the two lovers, joint by a strip with the writing *nunc et semper.*

The *Festival of Torrechiara* is held every year in July in the courtyard, with concerts and ballets. The Municipality of Torrechiara organizes it together with the *Academy of the Incogniti.*

Castle of Torrechiara
2: The courtyard of honour
3: One of the frescoed halls
4: The Golden Room
Page 154-155 - The imposing mass of the castle

5) MAGNANI-ROCCA FOUNDATION

It's located on the road reaching Traverse-tolo from Langhirano, in the locality called *Mamiano di Traversetolo*. It's a rich collection of paintings, sculptures and furniture spanning from the 12th century to now, displayed in a beautiful villa placed in the centre of a century-old park. The latter also accommodates a restoration place where typical products of the estates owned by the foundation can be purchased. The collection owes its existence to the enlightened generosity of *Luigi Magnani*, who lived between 1906 and 1984. The collection includes paintings by *Gentile da Fabriano, Filippo Lippi, Titian, Tiepolo, Rubens, Dürer, Van Dyck, Goya, Monet, Renoir, Cézanne, de Pisis, Morandi* and *de Chirico.* All the latter, coupled with sculptures by *Bartolini, Canova, Manzù* and furniture by *Thomire* and *Jacob* make this stop extremely pleasant and interesting. The premises also have at their disposal multipurpose halls for temporary expositions, concerts and meetings.

Magnani-Rocca Foundation
1: External view of the villa that is the seat of the museum.
2: Albrecht Dürer - "Madonna with Child" Oil on panel
3: Nicholas de Staël - "Vue des Quais de Paris" (1954) - Oil on canvas
4: Giorgio Morandi - "Still-life" (1942) Oil on canvas

5: Francisco Goya (1794) - The Family of the infant Don Luis" - Oil on Canvas

Continuous opening hours:
10 PM – 6 AM
Closed on Monday.
Closed in December, January and February.

6) MONTECHIARUGOLO

The village is near the road that leads to Tuscany and Liguria through the *passo di Lagastrello*.

The position was really strategic, and in 1406 *Guido Torelli* who had been invested with it by the Visconti decided to rebuild this powerful castle on a pre-existing one.

Later on, once it had become a property of the Farnese and the Bourbons, it was entirely changed into a gentlemanly residence.

It's possible to visit the watch communication trenches, a beautiful hall decorated with grotesques, the splendid balcony with elegant columns supporting the ceiling with wooden beams, and many frescoed rooms.

Just a few kilometres from Montechiarugolo it's possible to visit *Monticelli Terme*, a tranquil thermal resort whose *sodic bromo-iodic waters* were casually discovered by a farmer perforating the ground while looking for irrigation water.

1: *Montechiarugolo – The Castle*
2: *Motnicelli Terme: the Borrini Baths*

Three steps in the production of Parmesan Cheese:
3: *The curdling of milk*
4: *Marking*
5: *Maturing*

1